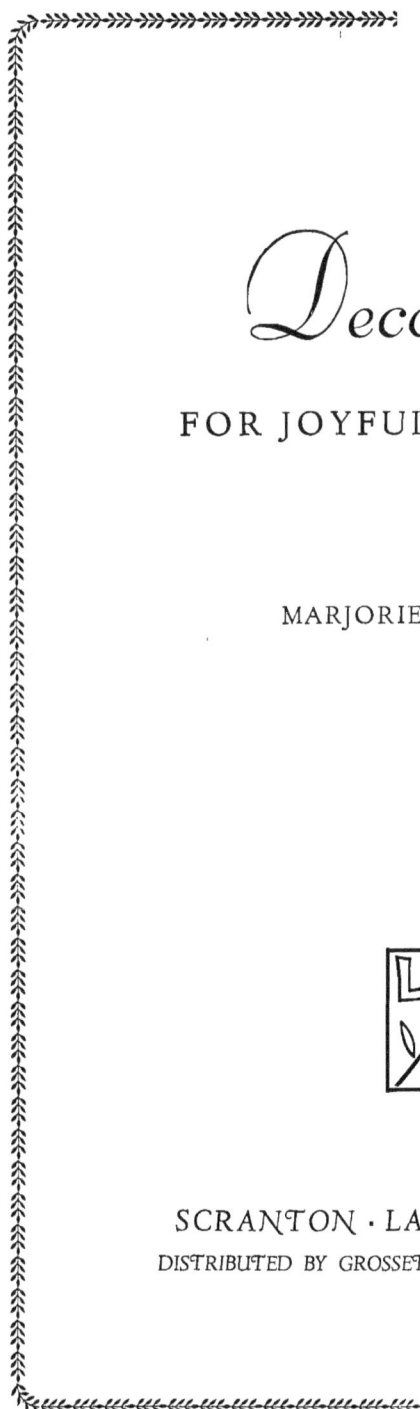

Decorating

FOR JOYFUL OCCASIONS

MARJORIE W. YOUNG

SCRANTON · LAUREL PUBLISHERS
DISTRIBUTED BY GROSSET & DUNLAP · NEW YORK

COPYRIGHT, 1952, BY INTERNATIONAL TEXTBOOK COMPANY
All Rights Reserved
Printed in the United States of America

FOREWORD

*P*EOPLE have been decorating to highlight the gaiety of some national or religious event since the beginning of time. The art of adorning and the art of making an ornament or trimming to symbolize a particular day have grown into a science. What you do to mark a holiday or create an atmosphere for some festive occasion is as important as what you wear or serve, or how you greet your guests and look after their comforts. You will probably be talked about favorably or otherwise as much from the standpoint of your decorating ideas as you will from your awareness of the latest fashions, your culinary skill, or your bearing as a hostess.

Marjorie Young, your author, knows a thing or two about decorating for joyful occasions, as she proves conclusively in this unique idea book, which covers inside and outside decorations and floral arrangements for holidays throughout the year. She has included new ideas, and unique variations of old ones, for all of the important holidays and for such other joyous occasions as bridal showers, weddings, wedding receptions, and church and club affairs. Her suggestions, her variations of old themes, will help you lend originality and sparkle to almost any type of entertaining you do. She will draw hidden talents from you (or your husband!), with her fresh, concise, practical "how-to" information.

Professionally Mrs. Young is a newspaper woman. Her extracurricular activities include free-lance magazine writing, the study of art, music, and cooking, and duties as a housewife. Decorating is one of her hobbies from which she has profited—and now you will too.

DRUCELLA LOWRIE, *Editor*

Marjorie W. Young

CONTENTS

1 MAKE HOLIDAYS IMPORTANT 3

2 CHRISTMAS 25

3 SPECIAL OCCASIONS 81

4 YOUR CHURCH AND CLUB 91

5 FLOWER AND TABLE ARRANGEMENTS 97

6 DECORATING FOR PROFIT 103

INDEX 119

1

MAKE HOLIDAYS IMPORTANT

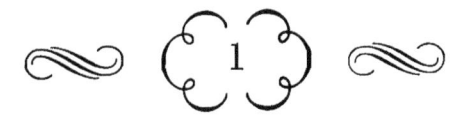

MAKE HOLIDAYS IMPORTANT

IF YOU let holidays and special occasions sweep you into a world of glamour, then this book was written for you! In it you will find decorating ideas that will lend originality and sparkle to almost any type of entertaining you might do.

NEW YEAR'S DAY

Suppose you're having a New Year's party. New Year's Day marks the beginning of a new year. It's a new page on which man eternally hopes to write a brighter story. You'll gather your relatives and closest friends around you to revive expectations for the future and to drink toasts to one another's health and prosperity.

Decorating for New Year's party. In decorating for your party, plan to have plenty of balloons, confetti, colored lights, streamers, and glitter of all sorts. Place mirrors in strategic spots so that the gay colors can be reflected. Bright red candles should be placed all around the room. At midnight you can turn off the electric lights and sing "Auld Lang Syne" to the flickering candles.

Across the mantel of the fireplace, tie bright letters spelling "Happy New Year." Hang tiny silver bells on strings of different lengths from each letter.

A cluster of balloons hanging from the center of the room will add to the gaiety and friendliness of the event.

Flower arrangements for New Year's Eve. For your centerpiece use white gardenias and flocked holly arranged in candle flower holders. A white-iced cake with its top decorated to resemble a clockface with the hands set to midnight would add to its effectiveness.

Twin flower arrangements in baby booties with a stork between them holding a baby doll marked 19― would be another suggestion.

New Year's decorations are more attractive when they are unusual, such as this arrangement of pink carnations, flocked carnation foliage, pine cones, and Christmas berries in a modern white container. (*Courtesy, Society of American Florists.*)

A very attractive centerpiece can be had by arranging carnations in a top hat container with colored paper streamers dangling down the sides. At each side use gold candles with carnation boutonnieres tied to them.

St. Valentine's Day

Red roses with rose foliage flocked, arranged in a white container, offer another idea. Set snowlady and snowman candles at each side.

ST. VALENTINE'S DAY

When the hilarity of New Year's wanes, St. Valentine's Day comes along in February to give dulling spirits a much-needed lift. St. Valentine's Day has long been a day set apart for all lovers to devote themselves to each other.

FIGURE 1

There are several stories about St. Valentine. In the reign of Claudius the Cruel, in Rome, Italy, there lived a priest by the name of Valentine who was popular with everyone. In those days war continued year after year and husbands did not want to leave their wives, nor lovers their sweethearts. When Claudius the Cruel sent forth a decree that there were to be no more marriages and all engagements were to be broken, people in love were so sad that Father Valentine married them secretly. When discovered, he was thrown into a dungeon by Claudius the Cruel. To honor his name after his death, people called February 14, the date of his birth, St. Valentine's Day. It became a day for exchanging love notes and gifts and also for marriages. The giving of flowers, particularly corsages, as living valentines, has become so widespread a custom that February 14 is one of the busiest days in the year for florists.

For Children

Children nearly always enjoy designing their own valentines. Supply them with gay-colored construction paper, scissors, paste, paper doilies, and scrap pictures. You'll be surprised at the results—some will be exceptionally clever!

Making a shadow box. The children can also make shadow boxes for their bedroom walls (see Figure 1). Figures in the box can be made of candy canes for legs, gumdrops for bodies, and marshmallows for heads.

To make the shadow box you will need:

- 1 box, picture-size
- 1 package of white lace paper doilies
- 1 red ribbon length the size of the four box sides
- 1 red satin ribbon for bow

For the two dolls, a boy and a girl, you will need:

- 4 candy sticks for legs
- 2 large gumdrops for bodies
- 2 marshmallows for heads
- 1 black gumdrop to be cut into small pieces for eyes, nose and mouth
- 2 small gumdrops for hats
- 2 5" lengths of satin ribbon for neckties
- 2 gumdrops to be sliced for shoes
- 1 box of toothpicks to hold the body together

Line the box with red paper. Cut the paper doilies in half and paste outside the box, leaving the large scalloped edges above the box. Tie red satin ribbon around outside of box, covering the cut bottoms of the paper doily.

Put a big red satin bow at the top. Punch a hole in the back of the box, 2" from the top, for hanging like a paper napkin box.

Place the dolls inside.

St. Valentine's Day   7

CENTERPIECES

A St. Valentine's party offers countless possibilities for centerpieces and favors. Since the heart is the symbol of the day, you might use gold-and-red hearts as a centerpiece.

Just like the reproduction of an old-fashioned lacy valentine. Such a beautiful table setting would bring forth oh's and ah's from party guests. The large nosegay centerpiece is composed of pink carnations, red roses, pink and white sweet peas, white freesias, blue irises, and white stevia, with miniature nosegays on streamers for party guests. The Dresden figurine of the dancing doll complements the arrangement in theme and color. The entire table setting has pink and red as its predominant colors, for pink and red are symbolic of love and St. Valentine's Day. (*Courtesy, Society of American Florists.*)

Cover two large cardboard hearts with red crepe paper and frame each with red cellophane ruffles that are fastened in place on the underside with Scotch tape. Cut out letters from gold paper spelling "I Love You" and paste them on the hearts. Stand the hearts against each other.

To make matching nut baskets, cover each nut basket with gold paper. Cut tiny red hearts and paste all around the middle of the basket. Trim the top of each basket with a lace paper doily.

Roses and violets are two favorite flowers for valentine centerpieces. Fill an old-fashioned slipper container with a nosegay of sweetheart roses and violets. Individual place cards should have rose and violet decorations on them.

Striped pink camellias attached to a vertical red satin heart and floating in a low container would make an effective table center. Place lovebird figurines at the side for added interest.

If in season, reddish pink tulips and heather with chenille hearts or hearts made of red-dyed pipe cleaners, arranged in a rectangular container with pink maline or taffeta shirred into a skirt around the container, could be used.

Pink callas in a white heart-shaped container would provide a dainty centerpiece for your table. Use pink heart-shaped nut cups at each place.

ST. PATRICK'S DAY

After the red-and-pink frills of St. Valentine's Day, we are greeted in March by the shamrock green of St. Patrick's Day. .

On March 17, A.D. 493, St. Patrick, who was the patron saint of Ireland, died. It is in his memory that St. Patrick's Day is dedicated.

Wearing o' the Green. The wearing of green carnations on St. Patrick's Day must have originated about the same time as the Mother's Day custom. However, as far back as the early 1890's, a Long Island florist surprised the public with green carnations. They caused such a sensation that they sold at a higher price than natural-colored ones. A combination of yellow and blue aniline dyes was his formula.

Although other flowers may be artificially colored, the carnation is the easiest to dye and green the easiest color to obtain. The long stems of fresh carnations are allowed to stand in water containing the dye, which is absorbed readily through the flowers' veins and

St. Patrick's Day

carried to the petals. The petals become a solid or striped color, depending on the variety of carnation. Powder dyes are also dusted on the carnations.

PARTIES

Favors and prize. Favors and place markers of green hats, shamrocks, or harps, as a prize for the best Irish song rendered by a guest, a green imitation snake will create a lot of fun and excitement.

Menu. Menu suggestions:

> Split-pea soup
> Fish or chicken with peas
> A fresh green salad
> Green tea, green ice cream, or lime sherbet
> Petite-fours with sugar shamrocks on the white frosting

CENTERPIECES

Floral centerpieces. If you are planning to use a floral centerpiece for your table, then, by all means, try to include the traditional flower of St. Patrick's Day in it.

You can place green carnations in a round white bowl with long-stemmed white stock or white carnations at the side to resemble pipestems.

An imitation harp can be made of heavy cardboard with wire or colored string for the harp strings. Place green shamrocks and green carnations around the base and here and there on the harp strings.

Paste green paper shamrocks on a white container and arrange, in the container, green and white carnations. Striped pandanus leaves can be used to surround the carnations. For added interest, a little doll dressed in a green costume can be set in the center.

Stovepipe hat. If you'd prefer not to use flowers as a centerpiece, an Irish stovepipe hat would be very attractive.

To make the crown of the hat, cut a piece of green cardboard about 12" by 36". Roll the two 12" ends together to form a cylinder. Stick in place with Scotch tape. The brim consists of two circles of green crepe paper pasted together. Fasten the brim to the crown with Scotch tape. Tie a white paper hatband around the crown and paste tiny green paper shamrocks around it. Smaller green hats or small clay pipes can be used as place markers and favors.

EASTER

The green of St. Patrick's Day is carried over into the Easter season as expressed in the arrival of spring flowers and in the awakening of the world to balmy breezes and warm sunshine. Yes, Easter is the season of rebirth—it is the queen of all Christian festivals. New bonnets and smiling faces announce the arousing of spirits to a fresh new world. Try to bring out this new freshness in your decorations.

MEALS

Brunch. Treat your friends to an Easter "brunch" right after church. Serve them on attractively decorated card tables covered with green crepe paper and crossed with yellow streamers. As a centerpiece for each table use a bowl of spring flowers surrounded by colored eggs.

Dinner. If you prefer to have your friends to dinner, you can make a charming "calla lily" centerpiece that will be certain to draw many oh's and ah's. Use a lace paper doily as the body of the calla lily. The iridescent stamens are made of bent pipe cleaners which have been dipped in glue and then in "flitter." ("Flitter" can be purchased in an art shop or hardware store.) Put the lilies in an Easter basket and surround them with lemon leaves.

EASTER TREE

Your children will love an Easter Tree dripping with fresh spring flowers, brightly colored Easter eggs, and miniature bunny rabbits. Garlands can be made of painted seeds or glass beads.

Secure the tree in a peck basket and tie the limbs to the handle. Weight the basket down with stones, covering them with a thick bed of green artificial grass. In the grass place bright-colored Easter

Easter 11

eggs. Tie a wide satin ribbon around the basket with a big bow. This tree can be used indoors or outside the house.

To make one tree egg. Prick a pin point at one end of a raw egg and make a hole about one-sixteenth of an inch in size at the opposite end. Put your lips lightly to the smaller hole and blow ever so

A beautiful floral arrangement for an Easter service. It consists of rubrum and Philippinense lilies. *(Courtesy, Society of American Florists.)*

gently and carefully so as not to crack the shell. The contents of the egg will flow out the larger hole.

You will need a hanger for the egg so that you can put it on the tree. Turn the eggshell on its side and with very little pressure (you must be careful or you will crack it) stick on tape. Attach a loop to each side. You will need an 8″ piece of ribbon for each loop.

Brush the egg lightly with Easter egg dye after you have hung it on the tree.

Flower Arrangements for the Table

The Easter season offers a large variety of flowers that will make lovely floral arrangements for your table.

Place yellow and white carnations in a glass basket. To one side you could set Mrs. Bunny wearing a little apron and a yellow carnation boutonniere on her head.

Yellow acacia and sweet peas make a lovely combination. You can arrange a bouquet of these in a Haeger bunny or in a lamb vase. Use Easter egg candles on each side.

What could be more suggestive of spring than yellow jonquils, tulips, and pussy willows? In a dark green container, a combination of these three will lend beauty to any table. Set a figurine of Pan or another symbol of spring at the side.

A flower girl and cart container can be filled with tulips, irises, Easter lilies, or jonquils.

White carnations and purple stock can be used to set off a purple-mottled pottery container. Place cards for this table arrangement can be made from Easter egg shells which have been made to look like pretty girls with hats on. (Their hats may be bits of paper doilies with flower petals on them.)

Into a striped Easter basket place yellow carnations and red and purple anemones. At the side, fluffy yellow chickens and colored Easter eggs can be used.

MOTHER'S DAY

In May mother receives her special recognition.

Anna M. Jarvis, of Philadelphia, originated the idea of Mother's Day in memory of her revered mother. On May 9, 1914, the first Mother's Day was proclaimed officially by Woodrow Wilson for observance on the second Sunday of May.

It became the tradition to wear red carnations in honor of living mothers and white ones in memory of those who had passed on.

Mother's Day

Gifts and decorations. This is one day mother may be pampered. Lavish upon her tokens of your love and affection. Here are a few suggestions that will enable you to make her day well worth remembering:

Cover a round bowl with powder-blue yarn. Inside, arrange pink roses, lilies of the valley, and irises. To the yarn ends, tie little gifts such as a pretty hankie, a small bottle of her favorite perfume, or a pair of gloves.

A double package for Mother and Father, wrapped in raspberry metallic paper and tied with blue satin and gold metallic ribbons. It displays a pink rosebud corsage with gold lace tied as on an old-fashioned valentine corsage. The lower gift is a perfume bottle tied with pink satin ribbons and blue forget-me-nots. (*Courtesy of Jensen.*)

If your mother likes to read, give her a pair of bookends that contain a special place for flowers. Foliage plants are very attractive in such a container, too.

Be sure that your gift to mother is beautifully wrapped, perhaps in a lovely, filmy scarf. If you use tissue paper and ribbon, you might tuck a flower in the bow.

Remember that this is your mother's own day. Make it festive!

FATHER'S DAY

June is Dad's month, for on the third Sunday father receives his treat—his own special day.

Mrs. John Bruce Dodd set this day aside in memory of her own father, who had successfully reared a family of children after their mother had died.

Gifts and decorations. In arranging for this occasion, try to get as much masculinity into your decorations as possible. Cater to Dad's favorite tastes—his hobbies or the things that he especially enjoys in his rare moments of relaxation.

If your father has a yen for fishing, then play up this theme in your centerpiece. Use a fishing basket as a container for red gladioli. (Red June roses or red peonies can be substituted in climates where gladioli are a late summer flower.) Scatter fishing flies here and there to lend atmosphere.

For a connoisseur of tobacco, a cigar humidor filled with peonies would be certain to get his approval.

Figurines suggesting Father's hobby can be used for many floral arrangements. You could use a jockey and horse, a porcelain sailboat, or pottery fish, for example.

A useful ice bucket can be dressed up attractively by placing red and yellow roses inside.

These are only a few ideas to help you think of many more of your own.

INDEPENDENCE DAY

The Fourth of July opens the gateway to summer and to the carefree, casual attitude that goes with it. It's the glorious day when people desert city streets and flock to picnics and outdoor parties.

Red, white, and blue are the color favorites of the day. Show your true patriotic spirit by making them prominent in your decorative scheme.

If you're entertaining at home, decorate the house with red and white crepe paper garlands. Cut these in 4" strips and twist.

Television party. This is a good evening for a television party. Your round stools could be made to represent firecrackers by covering them with red muslin and adding a white-and-black braided shoestring fuse in the center. For porch parties, these big firecrackers can be made out of nail kegs turned upside down.

CENTERPIECES

Your centerpiece should bring out the patriotic color scheme of the day. Set a large toy drum in the middle of a white tablecloth and surround the drum with blue candles. Run red or blue crepe paper streamers from the center of the drum to each place. As favors, cover little candy containers with blue crepe paper and stick a tiny flag on the far side with Scotch tape. Fill with red and white peppermint candies.

Gather up old mailing tubes, cover them with red paper, use braided ribbons for fuses, and BANG! you have another appropriate centerpiece.

If you have a floral centerpiece in mind, white carnations and blue bachelor's-buttons in a red vase would be colorful.

Blue and white delphiniums arranged in a low white container with a flag in the center are another idea.

If gladioli are in season in your locality, arrange some red and white gladioli in a blue vase and use red, white, and blue favors.

A three-tiered centerpiece with white flowers on top, red in the middle, and blue on the bottom would be very attractive. Place small Uncle Sam hats on either side.

HALLOWEEN

Every American has been well schooled in the history of Independence Day but few know the interesting origin of Halloween.

The Druids originated it centuries before the Christian era. November 1 was their New Year's Day and also the festival of their sun god. They believed that on the eve of this day the Lord of the Dead gathered together all the souls of the dead and decided what animal forms they should take for the next year.

Make Holidays Important

For us, October 31 has become an evening of "horrors" when ghosts and witches inhabit our neighborhood and knock on our doors for treats.

HALLOWEEN PARTY

A Halloween party is always fun. Let your imagination run wild when considering decorations. Keep your home dimly lighted. On

A witch centerpiece, including a witch, a ghost soufflé cup, a Halloween candleholder, and a cat decoration.

the lamp shades put black cats and witches. Lighted jack-o'-lanterns in dark corners will contribute to the weird atmosphere. Cobwebs made of light string or heavy thread will look realistic in the doorways. Here and there about the room scatter autumn leaves, cornstalks, and apples.

Refreshment table. On the refreshment table, perch a large jack-o'-lantern and rest it on a bed of leaves ringed with bright red

Halloween

apples. On each side, place two tall orange candles stuck in cored apples, cut flat on the bottom so that they will not roll. For favors, paste black cats or witches on nut cups that have been covered with orange crepe paper.

Bronze and yellow mums and pompons with Halloween table decorations chase away the spooks. (*Courtesy, Society of American Florists.*)

FLORAL ARRANGEMENTS FOR CENTERPIECES

Floral arrangements carry out the orange and black Halloween colors. Stuff a pumpkin container with yellow mums and use black cat accessories at the side of your centerpiece.

Paste black cats, bats, owls, and witches on a white pottery container and fill with white pompons. A black cat's head, made of paper, can be fixed so that it will peek around the back.

Another idea would be to cover a glass basket and handle with black crepe paper and arrange pompons, bittersweet, and wheat stalks inside. A paper witch astride some of the wheat stalks, the stalks resembling a broom, might be attached to the handle.

18   *Make Holidays Important*

Twin pumpkins filled with pompons and bittersweet would lend themselves to the Halloween atmosphere, as would white pompons and mums in a zebra-striped container. Some of these white pompons could be dyed black with the new flower dye which has come on the market.

This table setting is especially planned for football fans. Note the football-shaped container for the chrysanthemums, pompons, and roses, complimented by small football-shaped candleholders.   (*Courtesy, Society of American Florists.*)

THANKSGIVING DAY

Not long after the ghosts and goblins have gone into seclusion for another year, we are face to face with Thanksgiving preparations. Your decorations for this holiday should be just as snappy and brisk as the weather outside. Remember that your decorative ideas must compete with turkey-loving appetites; so they will have to be eye-catching.

Thanksgiving Day 19

Decorating the Table

Decorate the table with autumn leaves, ferns, or fruits arranged on a white linen tablecloth. Or lay a dark tablecloth in one of the new, modern weaves and use fiesta ware and gay colorful napkins. If you plan to have teen-agers as guests, decorate in the colors of

Suggested for a Thanksgiving buffet. There are yellow and bronze chrysanthemums, golden and rose-toned pompons, stalks of wheat, and yellow-marked croton leaves in a metal container with matching candleholders. (Courtesy, Society of American Florists.)

their school or college. You can use a novel container for the flowers.

A bunch of grapes, preferably blue grapes, can be used to create a frosty, sparkling centerpiece. Brush the grapes with unbeaten egg whites and then sprinkle with sugar. Place the bunch of grapes on a mirror and surround it with pretty autumn leaves.

Floral Arrangements for Table

Floral decorations such as the following will give your table a gracious and festive appearance.

Place Tritoma and yarrow in a copper container. Turkey figurines or candles will lend interest.

Fuji mums, sea oats, and bunches of beautiful grapes in twin arrangements make a Thanksgiving table especially festive. The gracious hostess also wears Fuji mums in her hair. (*Courtesy, Society of American Florists.*)

Brown cypripediums in a yellow container with yellow-mixed croton leaves, would be very effective.

Yellow roses, Chinese lanterns, and cattails in a copper container with Pilgrim figurines could be used.

Arrange red and orange Celosia, pompons of the same colors, and dried grasses with gourds and fruit in a cornucopia container.

Thanksgiving Day

A wooden cart container with pompons and artistic grape clusters is another suggestion.

Lavendar Fuji mums and red-marked crotons or the more formal Monstera deliciosa leaves can be arranged in a modern pottery container.

CHRISTMAS

CHRISTMAS

$\mathcal{O}$F ALL the holidays throughout the year, none has the universal appeal, excitement, and joy of the Christmas season. This annual church festival in memory of the birth of Christ is celebrated by most people on the twenty-fifth of December. It is a time of giving, receiving, and sharing the wonderful things associated with Christmas. There are the gifts, the festive dinner, the candy, fruit, and nuts, and the decorations indoors and out, and over all a deep sense of gratitude for the coming together of family and friends.

You have heard it said that children make Christmas, and it is true that the gaiety is on a slightly different plane when Santa Claus finds himself monopolized by them. However, Christmas is a day of rejoicing for everyone, and your decorations should be keyed to the warm feeling of hospitality and good will that is a part of the atmosphere at this time of the year.

The conventional and ever-popular decorations of holly, mistletoe, evergreens, berries, and red and green ribbon and paper are always associated with Christmas, but there are so many other colors and materials, perhaps more subtle than the red and green, that there is no end to the decorations you can create.

Because we in America are so decoration-minded, this part of our book has been written to give you a wealth of ideas for making your home the brightest and gayest spot possible at Christmas.

YOUR FRONT DOOR

Let us begin at your front door.

What will be more wonderful than an enormous wreath around your whole front door through which your friends can enter (see Figure 2)?

FIGURE 2

LARGE WREATH AROUND DOOR

Materials. You will need:

- 9 yards clothesline wire
- ½ bushel peat moss
- 5 large, well-shaped evergreen branches
- 9 large cloth poinsettia flowers
- 5 full-leaved magnolia branches. Rhododendron or mountain laurel leaf can be used if full-leaved magnolia branches are not available.

Your Front Door 27

    1 small can quick-drying red Chinese lacquer
    1 1" wide paint brush
    1 saucer household vegetable oil
  15 or more walnuts
    1 small can gold radiator paint or bottle of gilt
    2 spools florist's wire
    6 yards red oilcloth
    1 bunch florist's wooden picks
    1 card thumbtacks
    5 bushels of varying short-length evergreens

Any greens will last longer out of doors, but since hemlock and spruce are not good for indoors, you might like to use these for all your outside decorations. You may also want to remember, when choosing your greens, that laurel and bay are the emblems of triumph; that yew and cypress mean eternal life; and that ivy is for girls and holly for boys.

Frame for wreath. After getting your materials together you are ready to make your decorations. Take clothesline wire and form it into a circle. Be sure that you allow 2' between each side of the door and the wreath so that you will have no trouble opening and closing the door. Your door mat can be used as an anchor for the bottom of the finished wreath. Two nails driven into the wood above the door will be necessary for hanging the wreath. Drive them in at a place where the holes will not show later.

Tie the wire circle to a tree in your back yard, allowing the base to rest on the ground. Blanket the wire circle 1" thick with peat moss, wrapping with other wire to hold moss firmly in place. All your materials should be at your left, unless you are left-handed, so that you can work from left to right. It will go much faster that way.

Painting leaves and walnuts. Next, sort out half of the magnolia branches or the rhododendron or mountain laurel, as the case may be, making two separate groups. Wipe the leaves of one group with the vegetable oil, which cleans and polishes the foliage. Tie florist's picks to the branches where the leaves are fullest.

The other half of your leaves are to be painted red, for poinsettia petals. You will want to have them painted and dry when you need them. Brush them clean but do not oil them, and be sure the picks are tied firmly in place. These make good handles to hold while painting, unless you prefer to tie the leaves to a tree where they can hang to dry. If you cannot get the suggested leaves, buy the large-sized poinsettia flowers at a dime store.

Put a wire around each walnut as though you were tying a package and leave a 5" wire handle. Shake your can of gold or silver paint so that it is thoroughly mixed. Holding the walnuts by the wire handles, dip them into the paint, one at a time, and allow them to dry on a piece of paper in a basket so that they will not roll away.

Adding the greens. Pick up a bunch of evergreen clippings—about five, depending on their fullness—and hold them flat against the frame, pointing slightly to the right. Bind the wire around the stems very tightly, laying the spool down on the pie pan at each turn (so that it will not roll away) and picking it up on the other side.

When one bunch of greens has been tied to the frame, place another bunch a little below the first, pointing slightly to the left. From here on it is easy. Continue wiring the bunches on, turning them slightly to the left, then to the right, keeping them close together.

Tie small, full bunches onto a pick to fill in empty spaces, sticking the pick through the moss and wiring them on. Leave the bottom of the frame, which is on the ground, bare so that it will fit under the door mat.

Take the large boughs of evergreens, placing their wooded stems at the back of the wreath, and wire on firmly. Place the large, polished branches on the front side of the wreath, sticking the picks between the pine stems. When the red-lacquered leaves and the walnuts are dry, tie the gold nuggets in the leaf centers, placing them in groups around the wreath.

Red bow. Now you are ready for the big red bow. Cut off 12" of oilcloth. Divide it into two pieces to make the ends of the bow peeking out from under the door mat. Stick these to the mat with adhesive tape or tack them to the floor. Slit the remaining oilcloth lengthwise and sew together. Cut off another piece 10" long to use for the knot of your bow.

Your Front Door 29

Thumbtack the bow as low down on your front door as possible. Make sure the loop nearest the opening (at the doorknob side) is held quite tightly. Now hang the big evergreen wreath from the nails above your door and secure it tightly at sides and bottom by banding wire across it in several places and nailing this wire to the side of the house. This door wreath truly proclaims a greeting as joyful as your Christmas spirit and it says WELCOME to family and friends in a big way.

FIGURE 3

SMALL WREATH

All evergreen wreaths are assembled in much the same manner.

Materials. For the average-sized 18″ wreath (see Figure 3) you need:

      1 bushel evergreen cuttings 4″ to 6″ long
      1 circular frame
    2½ yards 4″ ribbon for bow
      1 spool florist's wire or very strong green cord
      1 bunch florist's sticks or picks

The frame. A branch of privet or willow makes a good frame. It can be bent easily without cracking. Overlap the ends and wire securely together. This will form a circle. For a smaller wreath you can bend a wire coat hanger into a circle; leave the hook on for hanging. A piece of heavy cardboard cut into a large ring is also good.

If you use a wire base it is best to wrap it in moss or strips of 1" cotton cloth (dark green is best) so that the evergreens will not slide.

The greens. The wreath will go much faster if you work on a table and place the basket of greens at your left. Hold the wire spool in your right hand, working from left to right—the scientific way to do all household chores.

Pick up a bunch of five or six evergreen clippings and hold them against the outside of the frame almost parallel, but pointing slightly to the left (northwest, compass-style). Wire on tightly. Lay the spool down on a pie pan or saucer at each turn so that it will not roll away. The next bunch of five or six clippings is placed just a little below the first, but pointing slightly to the right (northeast). Continue winding wire and adding greens until the base is completely covered.

The decorations. The trick of making a professional-looking wreath is to put all the decorations—such as cones, bows, and bells or balls—on individual florist's picks and to insert them after the basic wreath is finished.

Big red bows do a great deal to dress up a wreath. Be sure they are full enough, with plenty of loops. To make a nice bow, cut off a 30" piece of ribbon for ends. Take the remaining ribbon in your left hand, between thumb and forefinger. Now loop the ribbon back and forth, first to the right and then to the left, continuously, as you gather the loops tightly between your fingers, until finished. Wire the gathered center securely. Tie the 30" piece around the center, knotting at the back and allowing the ends to fall down to make streamers.

Your Front Door 31

Door Sprays

All you need:

>   5 full-needled pine boughs of various lengths
>   2 yards florist's wire
> 2½ yards 4" ribbon
>   2 handfuls pine tips
>   2 wooden picks

FIGURE 4

Divide the branches into two groups, the three longest boughs pointing their green ends to the right and the two shorter boughs pointing to the left.

Overlap the wood ends 3" and bind firmly together with wire.

Your spray can hang up and down or crosswise on your door. If it hangs widthwise on the door you will need two loops of wire 4" apart to hold it balanced. If it hangs up and down, three loops, one centered and two halfway out on the branches, should hold the spray in place.

Tie the ribbon bow on last, as you would in making the wreath.

Cover the bare spaces where the branches show above and below the knot of the bow with the two bunches of pine tips, which have been tied to florist's picks.

Spray for children. A spray which will amuse the children can be made with miniature wrapped packages, bells, and small store toys. Dangle them on ribbons from the center of a silver star. (See Figure 4.)

Materials. To make the spray you will need:

> 1 spray
> 1 8″ silver star
> 40 inches of 4″ red satin ribbon
> 16 miniature objects (toys and the like)
> 2 yards strong ½″ wide red ribbon

Making the spray. Punch two holes through the star, 1″ apart. Cut the narrow ribbon into eight different lengths. Thread the ribbons through the holes and tie or sew the miniature objects to the ends of the ribbons.

Cut the wide ribbon into five pieces, V-shaping the ends. Gather through the center with your fingers to make a pinwheel bow. Pinch the gathers together with a wire and tie to spray. Separate the ribbons so that they will appear from behind the V's of your star.

Bind the little ribbons together behind the star with a wire and bring the ends of the wire through the holes of the star. Cross over and down through the holes, as in sewing a button. Twist the wire again on the underside and fasten it securely onto the spray.

Children will have fun supplying miniature toys and wrapping "doll" packages for this decoration.

Star

A star is one of the most important Christmas decorations, since, as we all know, it was a bright star which led the Wise Men to Bethlehem where the Christ Child lay in his manger.

Your Front Door 33

Materials. To make the Swag Star shown in Figure 5 you will need:

>½ bushel balsam or arborvitae
>1 wire frame 6" in diameter (20" of wire)
>2 quarts peat moss
>1 tablespoon floral clay
>24 red glass balls
>1 bunch wooden picks
>Florist's wire
>3 yards green twine

FIGURE 5

Making the star. Make a wire frame 4" across and pad it with the peat moss to a thickness of about 2". Wrap the moss to the frame with strong green cord so that the frame will not show.

Place the evergreen branches upside down on a table top, with the leaf ends pointing out to form a five-pointed star. Now place the peat moss circle over the center of the wreath and wire each branch securely to the circle. Wire the inside stems together. Tie a wire across the back of the wreath in picture-frame style for easy hanging.

Turn the star over.

Place the red Christmas balls in a cloth-lined basket so that they will not roll away. If there is a ring in the end of each ball, remove it, and replace it with a pick tipped with floral clay. If the balls have wire stems, use three at a time, wrapping the wires about the pick.

FIGURE 6

Once the balls are complete with picks, stick them into the peat moss. The balls which cover the center hole (3″ to 4″) need to be held in place by wiring through the back of the wreath.

Hang this gay star on your door, or in the center of a big space between the windows, or over your living room mantel, where it will say a shiny, sparkling "Merry Christmas!" to all your holiday visitors.

Your Front Door

JOLLY FRONT DOOR DECORATION

You will know there are children waiting for Santa Claus behind this jolly front door decoration. And what fun it will be for them to help put it together! To make this door decoration (Figure 6) cut out happy children's faces from magazine covers or posters.

Materials. You will need, in addition to the faces:

>Colored glass balls
>Red cardboard
>Glue
>A package of tinsel dust or a bottle of gold paint
>Small empty boxes, Christmas-wrapped
>2 little pine tree branches
>Inexpensive toys (doll furniture, horns, cars, and so on)

Making the decoration. Sort through old magazines or posters with the children and have them select faces which resemble members of your family, especially in the coloring of hair and eyes.

Cut out these family "portraits" to shoulder length and paste them to the bottom of the windowpane, on the inside. Paste a strip of red paper 3" high across the bottom to hold them together as a group. For the streamer beneath the portraits, cut a strip of red cardboard 9" wide (you may need to paste two pieces together) and about 1 yard long.

Have all the family members sign their names on the cardboard —as large as they can—in pencil, writing one name underneath another (see Figure 6 again). Leave about 3" of space between each pair of names.

Using a rubber-top glue bottle, go over the names, or brush the glue over the names, so that the sticky liquid outlines the letters. Quickly dust the tinsel powder over the wet glue. Dust plenty of powder on, as the wind may take some off when the streamer is tacked outside. Gold paint can be used instead of tinsel, but it is not quite as effective.

This banner of names should be thumbtacked securely to the door, top and bottom, just below the door window.

String a necklace of glass Christmas balls on sturdy cord or thin wire and make a frame for the window. Tack a short nail, slanting outward, at each of the four corners of the window. Between the balls, about every 4", thumbtack a small piece of cloth across the necklace. This will hold it in place.

Make a "Merry Christmas" sign to place at the top of the door window. Produce it in the same way as the family name banner, with pencil, glue, and tinsel dust.

FIGURE 7

Trees for each side of door. Lastly, you make the decorations for each side of the front door. Fashion small trees out of pine boughs, unless you are lucky enough to have some trees already planted. Decorate the trees with inexpensive store toys, rainproof if possible, in bright colors. Use little bells, animals, and doll-sized boxes wrapped in gold and silver paper with red bows. Each child can also add one miniature of a toy he wants for Christmas, and an article he hopes to give to some other child.

Finally, top each tree with a sparkling star.

Your Hall Stairway 37

YOUR HALL STAIRWAY

Magnolia or Rhododendron Branches

If you have a large hall stairway, one of the most beautiful holiday decorations can be made by taking magnolia or rhododendron branches and weaving them through your stair railing posts, tying them on securely. Polish the leaves with oil before starting. Buy a long string of light sockets, larger than tree size, and place them in

Figure 8

the heavy parts or center of the foliage. White light bulbs show up best and give the most light. Add several extra leaves around each bulb to form a flower effect. Tie a large red bow to the end of the newel post or hand railing. (See Figure 7.)

Materials. For this stairway decoration you will need:

   2 spools florist's wire
   20 frosted light bulbs
   4 yards wide red satin ribbon
   2 electric cords with base plugs, with 10 sockets each—one for the upstairs plug and one for the downstairs plug
   15 branches of magnolia. If you cannot get magnolia branches, use any of the pine boughs which do not shed their needles.

Make small wreaths of the magnolia branches and place the light bulbs through their centers. Good evergreens for indoors are arborvitae, laurel, rhododendron, taxus, Scotch pine, ilex, balsam, and juniper. Hemlocks shed their needles in a heated house and should be used only out of doors. Mix your greens, the broad-leaved with the coniferous, to give contrast in texture and beauty.

Musical Stairway

If your stairway is at the side of your living room, a "musical" decoration would be interesting and appropriate. Your balustrade (see Figure 8) can be turned into a "pipe organ"—with angels "singing" a greeting as one goes up and down the stairs.

Materials. You will need for your musical stairway:

- 15 mailing tubes, or more or less, according to the number of banister posts
- 7 sheets of gold paper. Or paint the tubes with gold paint. Short piece of florist's wire to attach bow to post
- 1 piece of printed music
- 3 tinsel stars
- Wire for a large and small halo
- 4 yards of wide green satin ribbon
- 2 red Christmas bells

Construction. The pipe organ is easily made. Ordinary mailing tubes can be either painted gold or wrapped with gold paper. Slit them lengthwise on one side with a sharp knife; this is done so that you can slip them over the individual railings. You may have to cut each tube in two pieces in order to get it over with ease, but this will not matter, since you can paste them together again before they are covered with the gold paper or paint. Cut a small triangular-shaped hole in the front of the tube, about one-third up from the bottom; this gives the effect of the opening in the pipe through which the sound comes. Starting with a full-sized mailing tube at the center of your stairs, cut the tubes lower and lower, slanting them at the bottom toward the front edges of the stairs. Leave the last two feet of banister free for your angel.

Take the cardboard from a laundered shirt and draw the outline of a paper doll—head, neck, shoulders, arms, waistline, and skirt.

Your Hall Stairway

Cut it out along your pencil lines. With another piece of cardboard make triangles. Round the edges of one corner. This will form the wings. Sew the wings to the body.

Wet the angel with glue from the waist up and dust with gold powder. While this is drying make a pleated skirt from a piece of gold paper. This can be tied on around the waist with a blue ribbon when shoulders and wings are dry. Pin a piece of sheet music in the angel's hands.

FIGURE 9

Loop a 1" heavy ribbon between the gold pipes, attaching this securely to the back center of each pipe. This gives a professional touch to the organ.

Place silver stars above your angel, on the hand rail and the banisters. Between the stars and head float a small gold halo on thin invisible wires.

Tie a large green satin ribbon around the neck of your newel post. Two large red bells hung from the bow will add to the musical stairway. Place on top of the newel post a gold halo made of wire and wrapped with gold paper.

Hide a little music box on the stairway in a spot where it can be turned on at a moment's notice. If it plays Christmas carols, so much the better. You may be sure that this delightful musical arrangement will so please your friends that they will sing your praises for months.

YOUR ENTRANCE HALL

Miniature Pipe Organ on Table

If your entrance hall is small, a miniature pipe organ (Figure 9) can be made and placed on a little table. This should form a part of a floral decoration.

Materials. You will need:

> 9 mailing tubes or bamboo pieces
> 4 pieces of gold paper or gold paint for the tubes
> 1 graceful pine branch
> Cornstarch or flower for branch paint
> 1 bowl for greens
> 1 silver tray
> 3 porcelain or candle choir boys

Making the pipe organ. Cover the table with a piece of red velvet. Take a silver tray—if you can spare one at Christmas time. Arrange a bowl of fine-leaved greenery at one side of the tray. Take a thinly branched evergreen which has been painted white (you can mix flour and cornstarch with water for this white "paint"). Curve this painted branch around and over the pipe organ. Pin or wire onto it small white artificial Christmas roses. Tinseled silver stars may be used instead of the flowers, or you can cut paper roses out of wallpaper with small patterns.

Place three porcelain figures of choir boys on the tray in front of the pipe organ. If you find porcelain figures unavailable or too expensive to use, you might like to use little candle choir boys.

A small spotlight throwing its beam over the scene will seem to increase the size of your hall.

Wall Decoration

If your hall is too small for a table, why not use a wall decoration?

Your Entrance Hall 41

Bells or something metallic over greenery, with the addition of bright ribbon, can be most effective.

Good luck piece. Why not make the "something" metallic a good luck piece—such as an old horseshoe shining with gold paint, as in Figure 10. Be sure the ends are pointed up, to hold the "good luck" captive within the shoe. Tie a bright-colored ribbon around the horseshoe, like a ribbon around a box of fancy candy. Choose a

FIGURE 10

ribbon which will make a nice contrast with your hall colors. Place the horseshoe in the center of a small spray.

If you cannot find a real horseshoe, make one out of cardboard and cover it with gold paper. Punch large holes through the center around the bend. Draw different colors of ribbons through the holes and stick a flower of a contrasting color in each hole. This is truly beautiful if placed under a hall light.

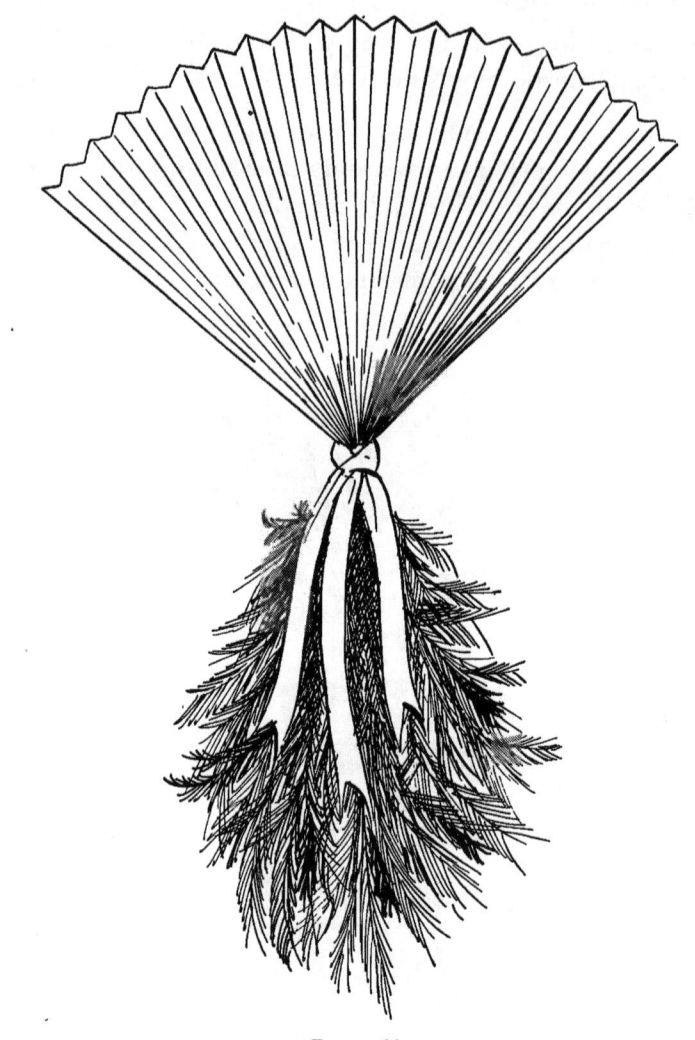

FIGURE 11

You will need:

>   1 horseshoe, or any brass object such as a French horn
>   1 spray
>   1 2″ red or bright-colored ribbon or
>   9 18″ pieces of ribbon of various colors

Gold fan. A narrow hall can be highlighted at one end by a gold fan tied at the handle end to a bunch of pine boughs (see Figure 11).

Your Entrance Hall

Materials. For this hallway fan decoration you will need:

    40 inches of 12" wide gold paper
    3 yards of 2" wide ribbon
    5 inches of Scotch tape
    Florist's wire
    ½ spray (bottom)
    Cornstarch tinted with vegetable coloring or bluing

Making the fan. To make this fan, take a piece of gold paper 40" long and 12" wide. You will probably need to paste two pieces together to get the desired length. Fold the paper over a ruler, back and forth, making 1" folds. Press down hard with the flat of your hand and turn up one end about 1½". This will make the handle of your fan. Secure this with Scotch tape. Your pine boughs can be tinted by painting them with, or dipping them into, a mixture of cornstarch and water tinted with vegetable coloring. Wire the tinted pine boughs and form a hook at the back.

Take a small stick the size of half a yardstick and wire this to the back of the spray. Allow it to extend up as high as the top of the fan. Thumbtack the center of the fan to the stick.

Braid three strips of 2" wide ribbon around the place where the fan joins the pine. Let them hang down, streamer-style.

This decoration for walls would be charming used between two hall lights, or as a decoration under or over mantelpiece lights or dining room lights.

Evergreens

Evergreen wreaths, sprays, or branches set off with a big red satin ribbon bow always seem to radiate a welcoming appeal. Of these, there is nothing quite as symbolic as holly. Remember the old saying, "Whoever brings the first sprig of holly into the house at Christmas rules the home for the coming year." In the early days holly was considered hateful to witches and a charm against lightning. Thus it has come to mean protection against evil, to have holly about the house.

Ivy has always been the symbol for the wine god Bacchus. It is not used inside the house, but it can be used outside.

In many countries, placing the evergreens in the house before Christmas Eve is considered unlucky. And, oddly enough, most superstitions are based on sound reasoning. People probably used the "unluckiness" theory to keep greens out of the house so that they would not become dry and highly inflammable. We know that to make the house a fire hazard by having it full of dangerously dry greens *could* be unlucky.

Custom dictates that greens should be removed by Twelfth-night, or before Plow Monday. The people of some countries believe that greens should be burned on Candlemas Eve, while those of other countries believe that they should be left in the yard to decay.

Your Christmas tree can be shared with the birds when you wish to remove it from the house. After the decorations are put away for another year, why not set your tree up outside? Tie suet and raisin balls on it for the birds' delight. They will also enjoy popcorn strings and cranberry necklaces if left on the tree.

Mistletoe. The mistletoe must hang overhead in every front hall at Christmas, so that the moment your threshold is crossed, each holiday guest can be greeted with a surprise kiss of Christmas cheer and welcome.

For use in the home, mistletoe should be bunched in a round formation, and hung at least 8' from the floor. It should be suspended from a wire or ribbon, and should always have a red ribbon tied over its stumpy stems.

A jolly decoration can be made by hanging snowballs on thin wires from the mistletoe. These can be purchased or cut from white foam plastic.

The use of mistletoe at Yuletide dates back to an old Scandinavian custom: if enemies met in the forest beneath mistletoe, by mistake, they laid down their arms until daybreak. Thus, mistletoe seems always to have played the role of bringing people together in amiable spirits and good fellowship.

According to another legend, the white mistletoe berries are the tears of the Goddess of Love, Freyja. It seems that between the last leaf of fall and the first bud of spring, her son Balder used to carry

Your Living Room 45

A fine example of a beautiful modern Christmas tree. It is sprayed with ordinary aluminum paint. The balls are green and gold, and two baby spotlights are used, one of green gelatin and the other of gold gelatin. (*Courtesy of Bob Jones University.*)

a spray of mistletoe on the tip of his spear. Because it is the only plant which stays green the entire year, the carrying about of mistletoe indicated that love is stronger than death.

YOUR LIVING ROOM

The Christmas Tree

Now we are ready for your living room and its important Christmas decorations.

Germany gave us the custom of decorating an evergreen tree. The Christmas tree put in its appearance in the eighth century, when

Boniface, a missionary, replaced pagan sacrifices of food by a decorated fir tree. He placed a silver star as high as it would go on the tree, in tribute to the Christ child, and there its bright promise radiated to all the world a new hope for mankind.

There is nothing which lends more to the holiday spirit than a large Christmas tree. The old-fashioned American Christmas tree was a green pine tree with a star at the top. Today many Christmas trees are painted or sprayed in light pastel tints; others are gilded.

The gaily painted walnuts which hung from the branches are now replaced by colored glass balls and plastic toys. Lighted candles sparkled on the trees in those days, but we find electric tree lights less hazardous and equally pretty. Cotton is now fireproofed for added safety. All precautions are taken to insure a safe as well as a spirited Christmas season.

Your tree must be placed away from heat and out of the pathway of doors. Of course you will want to share it with those who pass by, so we suggest placing it near a window if possible. It will shine out its colorful, friendly greeting to all.

Inside Doorway Decorations

Christmas cards in oilcloth holders. Christmas cards make a happy decoration around an open doorway. They are so gay and personal. Why not make oilcloth holders for them? Red oilcloth would be effective. You can make two different kinds—one with pockets or one with slits, like the old-fashioned post card album, for holding the cards.

To make the one with pockets for one side of the doorway, measure the height of your doorway, which is probably 6'. Add half of this length to make pockets. The strip of oilcloth should be 5" wide. Start making folds at the bottom of the strip. These should be 2" deep and $5\frac{1}{2}$" to 6" apart. Make pockets the full length of the oilcloth strip.

Press the oilcloth to keep it in place until you stitch it on the sewing machine to hold it permanently. This makes a long strip of small pockets just deep enough for your cards to peek from.

Your Living Room 47

It's a bright holder to display all your incoming greeting cards, and it makes a very colorful and personal decoration for your room. You'll find it quite a conversation piece too, as your friends gather around to exclaim over your many and varied greetings.

Top the door with holly branches so that their red berries will carry color across your doorway.

If you do not wish to go to the trouble of sewing pockets, make the strip with slits. Measure the length of one side of the doorway, and make a 5" wide strip of oilcloth. In it cut small slits into which the corners of your cards will fit. You may want to stagger your cards to right and left on the strip. Since cards vary so much in size, you may cut the slits for them as they are put in place, rather than before. If so, hold the card against the oilcloth and mark on it the bottom left corner of the card, then mark the upper right corner. Cut 2" slits through which the corners of the card will fit.

If you receive many greeting cards, two strips of oilcloth will not be enough to hold them all. Make more and hang them side by side along the wall.

If the edges of your oilcloth tend to curl, or you want to give the strips a more finished look, gold ribbon can be stitched along the outside edges.

These oilcloth strips are nice carry-overs from one season to the next, provided you store them where it is not too warm, and roll them with wax paper between the folds.

Cards fastened with cellophane tape. You can frame the doorway with cards taped to the casing with cellophane tape.

Cards hung from tree. Some people punch a hole in the top of each card and hang the cards from the tree with colored yarn or twine.

AT THE WINDOW

Balls and stars across window. Any window not too near the tree could lend a festive air by displaying bright balls and tinsel stars strung on wires X-shaped across it. (X stands for the first letter in the Greek word for Christmas, from which we get the shortened form *Xmas*.)

To hold this X in place, it would be well to have two thin pieces of wood at the sides of the window so that you will not mar the wood of your frame.

Outside crèche. For the window beside the tree, use an outside crèche (*crèche,* pronounced "krash," is the name for the manger scene). If you are fortunate enough to have a window box there, or an extra-wide window sill, so much the better. This crèche will look well from either the outside or the inside of your house.

To make the crèche, use a small wooden box 8" to 10" long. Take off one of the larger sides and place it on top of the box, making a slanting roof. Build a little manger of crossed sticks and fill with straw. Place this inside the wooden box. Buy (unless you are clever enough to make them) small figures which represent Mary, Joseph, the Infant Jesus, shepherds, the Magi, and some animals, such as sheep, cattle, donkeys, and camels. Fasten these figures securely to the board by wiring them around the middle and the feet. Add a layer of cotton to the roof of the crèche.

If your Christmas tree is located in the window behind your crèche, its star will look like the Star of Bethlehem from the street. It would be well, however, to paste a silver star on the inside of the windowpane, to be seen when the Christmas tree star is not in view.

Crèche in fireplace. If you are not going to use your fireplace for burning wood or coal, this is another excellent location for a crèche.

Line the inside of your fireplace with light blue crepe paper. Paste stars around the top half. Use brown crepe paper for the earth, and build a little manger like the one described. Since this crèche is indoors, there is no need to use cotton. Sticks pasted on the roof will give an authentic effect.

BETWEEN LIVING ROOM AND DINING ROOM

Garland over doorway. How about a garland over the doorway between your dining room and living room? String ornaments on

Your Living Room

a wire or cord and tie bows between the balls to keep them 3" or 4" apart.

Hang this garland across the doorway and tie the center up to the top, to form a loop on either side. Another way to dress the door would be to float foam snowballs from invisible wires tacked onto the door frame before the garland is hung in place.

House plants. If you have house plants, they too should be cleaned and dressed up with bows and fancy tinsel papers tied around their pots.

Holly wreaths. Holly wreaths are a must at Christmas because of the tree's association with the Crucifixion. According to the legend, the crown of thorns came from "branches which bore white berries." After the Crucifixion, however, according to legend, the berries of this tree became red. Today they are known as holly.

Homemade holly and evergreens. You do not need to go out and buy real holly for your wreaths. Make them out of cardboard or paper plate rims wrapped in green crepe paper and ornamented with bunches of cranberries. For gold wreaths, get a bottle of radiator paint and let the children join in the fun.

To take the place of evergreen garlands for your doorway, dye yards of cheesecloth green and hide bright balls in its folds. You can make these balls by covering walnuts or paper balls with various colors of metal papers and tin foil from cigarette packages.

Room Decorations

"Dress up" various objects about the room to echo the Christmas spirit.

Sofa pillows. Tie a large red bow on the corner of one or two sofa pillows.

Wastebaskets. Wastebaskets, which are generally forgotten, can be covered with Christmas wrapping paper tied on with a contrasting ribbon.

Gift table. Set up a gift table in the living room. This would be lovely with a lavish cover garlanded with greens and ribbon. As a background, a small felt or cardboard Christmas tree tacked against the wall would give the feeling of "presents under the tree" (see Figure 12). Name tags would need to be sealed in small envelopes until Christmas Eve or hidden under the packages. This

FIGURE 12.

gift table could be used for your own presents after the "grand opening."

Floor lamp. The base of your floor lamp can be turned into an imitation candy cane by wrapping its long stem with 4" wide strips of red and white crepe paper.

Pair of table lamps. If you have a pair of table lamps, baste a paper wreath around the top of each shade. Another way to dress your table lamps for Christmas is to encircle their bases with a

Your Living Room   51

wreath (see Figure 13). These wreaths are very effective, especially when the lights are turned on over them.

Desk. If you have a desk in the living room, keep its working surface free but decorate above or down the sides. On the free working surface put a large copper bowl filled with pine cones; this makes an attractive decoration. Arrange a few short branches of pine in the middle so that their needles will not fall outside the

FIGURE 13

bowl. A large copper or brass tray behind the decoration will reflect its beauty. Your copper can be polished quickly by rubbing it with a piece of lemon rind and salt.

Room walls. If the walls of your living room are painted in a dark shade, use light-colored wreaths and garlands or gold or silver ones. With a dark green or brown wall, use either white or gold wreaths.

For gray walls nothing is so lovely as shiny wreaths of Christmas red, especially when tied with a large white or silver bow.

Mantel. *Mantel trees.* Mantel trees make a lovely decoration (see Figure 14). They are also good in a room with limited space.

Branches cut from a shrub or tree can be painted any color or gilded to contrast with the colors on your walls. The boxes which hold the trees should be painted the same color as the tree; they are lovely when banded with contrasting ribbon or tape. These containers hold the trees well in place if they are filled with moist sand or cinders. The trees should be trimmed with miniature decorations, which at a distance will give the effect of seeing a large tree in full

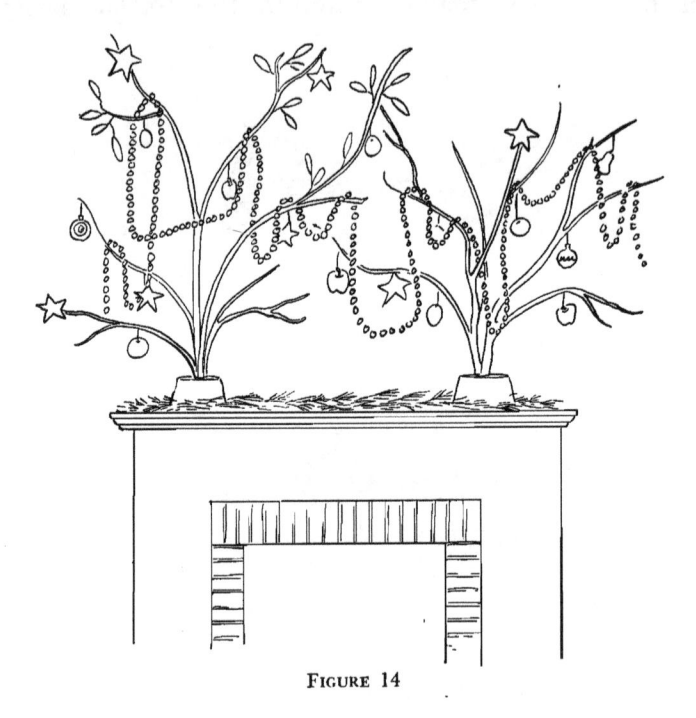

FIGURE 14

fruit. Glass balls, cranberries, small stars, cones, tiny apples, miniature toys, and little candy canes make good decorations. Bank your mantel board with evergreens to give the effect of grass under your tree.

A mantel tree made with bits of greenery such as twigs of balsam, Scotch pine, taxus, laurel, or spruce, complemented with only one kind of fruit (hanging on invisible wires) such as cranberries, limes, or lemons, makes a modern-style decoration.

Gold fan on mantel. Another suggestion would be to decorate the mantel with a large gold fan. Edge the fan with white lace

Your Living Room 53

paper doilies and tie contrasting green ribbon streamers at the handle end. Place small, bright-red apples in cellophane bags and attach these to the ends of the streamers, allowing them to hang over the mantel to give an ultramodern effect.

Fisherman's mantel. A fisherman's mantel (Figure 15) can be made with two bamboo rods, a line, sea shells, coral, feather flies,

FIGURE 15

lures, and silver stars. Cover the front of the chimney mantel with dark blue-green fireproof material to protect the rods from heat. Place the handles of the rods in the palm of a glove and stand in a tackle box on the right side of your mantel. Decorate the mantel shelf with greens, and place an aquarium of goldfish at the left. Brace the sea shells and coral along the mantel, filling its entire width as though it were under water.

With fishline, tie lures, flies, and small silver stars along the nodes of the rods. If you do not have an old fishing line which can be cut into small pieces, just loop and tie the line, Navy-style, so that it will not tangle. Add a few strings of bright-colored glass beads to your bait. The heavier objects should be on the small ends of the poles so that they will curve the bamboo. A few pieces of

FIGURE 16

green smilax caught in the line will give the underwater "algae" look.

This would be a different way of presenting a gift of new equipment to your favorite fisherman.

Christmas Flower Arrangements

Here are some suggestions for Christmas flower arrangements:
Place white carnations, gilt pine cones, and variegated holly in a bronze container. Surround it with snow family candles.

Your Powder Room

Crisscross candy canes in the middle of an arrangement of red carnations and pine. A red ribbon bow may hold the candy canes together.

Red roses, white mums, and a frosty candle will look attractive in a low container, especially if you add red and gold ornaments for brilliance.

Arrange red and white poinsettias around a Santa Claus candle. A graceful arborvitae may be flocked or gilded.

Santa Claus boots with white mums and holly would lend a festive note to your table.

Decorate a miniature tree with white gardenias or red and white camellias. Underneath arrange a skating scene with a mirror, bits of sparkly cotton around the edge, and ice-skating figures.

A miniature tree made entirely of red and white carnations, in a green satin bucket, would be effective.

YOUR POWDER ROOM

For your powder room, make two small Christmas trees (Figure 16) out of white crepe paper dotted with red and green spangles and gummed stars. These will go on your dressing table. Each tree will stand in an angel food cake pan filled with colored glass balls.

To make one powder room tree you will need:

- 3 lace paper doilies
- 3 pieces 20" x 40" white crepe paper
- 1 box each red and green gummed stars
- ½ bottle red and green spangles
- 1 angel food cake pan
- 18 colored glass balls, according to size of tree
- 5" wide white satin ribbon—two pieces the length of one width of your mirror, and one "wreath" bow
- 1 cup putty or clay
- 2 dozen white ball powder puffs
- 10 yards (total) red and green satin baby ribbon

Make a garland of wide white satin ribbon, with a large bow in the center, to put across the top and down the sides of your mirror. From the bow over the mirror, hang red and green satin baby ribbon streamers. Tie white powder puffs (cotton snowballs) to their ends.

To make the trees: Take three 12" lace paper doilies, circular in shape. Cut three strips of white crepe paper 20" wide, with the grain, and 40" long. Fold to a 10" width for the tree branches.

To make the tree trunk: Take a small round stick 20" long (a long wooden spoon handle will do) and stick one end into a ball of

FIGURE 17

putty or clay. Flatten the bottom before it is dry so that the tree will stand up straight. Place the trunk inside the hole of the angel food cake pan.

Gather the 40" crepe paper branch, where it is doubled, by shirring the paper over a knitting needle. Replace the knitting needle with spool wire. Gather and pull it firmly around the bottom

Your Dining Room

of the tree trunk, 9" from the rim of the pan. With your fingers ruffle the crepe paper edges.

Punch a small hole in the middle of a paper doily and cut from this doily a pie-shaped quarter section. Use the three-quarter section remaining and ruffle its edges like pie crust. Paste or tape together by lapping over 1" more or less, as required. Slide doily down over the stick until it meets the branch you have just wired on. Complete the tree and fill cake pan with ornaments.

YOUR DINING ROOM

Your dining room is one of the most important places in your home at Christmas time. It is here that a large part of your sharing of the Season's joys takes place.

Planning the decorations. It might be wise to have a notebook for jotting down all the wonderful decoration plans you will make for your holiday dining.

First make a rough sketch of empty wall space—the space, for example, on each side of the buffet, or a spot between windows or doors. You may even want to take down a picture or two to make more room on the wall for seasonal decorations. Note this in your book.

Wall Christmas Trees

Whether your dining room is large or small, two wall Christmas trees (Figure 17) will give your home that quality of being well loved, and like that of a good housekeeper, well planned.

These trees can be used in any small apartment or in the living room, bedroom, or hall. They take up almost no space, but are a beautiful decoration.

The trees are made of chicken wire with short branches of pine, a star, bright glass balls, tinsel, and red ribbon cascades. If you live in a tropical country where you cannot get chicken wire, a fish net can be substituted. If you have no pine, cut a tree out of heavy paper and paint it green. The bright balls and cascades will make it look like a real Christmas tree.

Materials. You will need, for one tree:

- 7½ feet of 40″ large-mesh chicken wire
- 1 pair of wire clippers
- 64 inches of clothesline wire
- 2 large screw eyes
- 1 nail for wall behind star
- 1 2″ metal ring
- 1 star
- 1 cascade of tinsel or cellophane
- 1 cascade of ¾″ wide red satin ribbon
- 6 bushels of pine clippings
- 2 spools of florist's wire or strong green string
- 1 7½′ piece of ½″ thick wood

Making the tree. To make the wall Christmas tree, lay the chicken wire flat on the floor. Tie a long piece of string on the left side of the chicken wire 18″ up from the bottom. Stretch the string up to the top center of the wire (this will be about 20″ in from each side). Tie the string firmly to the center wire. This is where your star will go later. Now bring the string down the right-hand side of the wire and tie it in the same manner, 18″ from the bottom. This string is used only as a measuring device or guide for the pattern of the tree outline. Wire or nail a 7½′ wooden stick ½″ thick, down the center of your frame.

Take another piece of string and curve it downward from the ends of the first string, allowing its center curve to dip down within 14″ of the bottom of the wire. Tie this on at several spots so that it does not lose its curved space while you work.

To make the tree trunk, mark the center of the wire at the bottom and measure off 3″ on each side, allowing the trunk to curve out, root-style, toward the bottom.

Now you are ready to cut out your tree, and it may be best for you to use an old pair of leather gloves to protect your hands when cutting wire. Cut along the lines of your chicken wire where indicated by the string—leaving a little extra wire, rather than a little less, along the markers.

With a basket of greens at your left hand, start tying them on, starting at the center top and working down. Cut the florist's wire or green string into 2″ lengths. You will be surprised how fast this

Your Dining Room

tree will shape up for you. Use a pillow or mat for kneeling above the wire.

Placing the tree. You are now ready to hang the tree from one good strong picture nail which has been driven into the wall 7' from the floor.

After the tree is on the wall, make a large X across the tree with wire; this will keep it from curling forward. The wires can be attached or secured to any available woodwork, such as a window or doorway. Fluff out any small branches under the wire. Hang your brightest Christmas balls on the tree branches.

Cut the red satin ribbon into pieces 18' long. Take the ribbon streamers and draw them through the 2" metal ring. Tie each one onto the circle. Slip the ring over the nail at the top of the tree and let the ribbons cascade down.

Take the star and attach the tinsel or cellophane cascade to the back of the star, and wire it securely onto the same nail.

Now you have come to the last step. Take the clothesline wire and form a half circle about the base of the tree, extending it out as far as the widest branch. Bend the ends into a circular hook and attach to screws which have been previously screwed into the bottom of the wooden baseboard of your room. This wire should curve out over the floor, making a "new moon" shape. The distance between the baseboard and the widest part of this semicircle will be 14". This protects the tree.

Sort out the red ribbon streamers, and with the satin sides toward you, tie them onto the floor wire. This arrangement gives a straight outline to your decoration. Besides being luxurious, it protects your tree.

(Small wall trees can be cut out of felt and thumbtacked to the wall, the balls being sewed on first. Top the shiny tree with the star, and make small red satin streamers. If you intend to use this small wall tree on a side table, the streamers can be thumbtacked to the underside or taped in place.)

Table and chairs. With this elaborate wall decoration your dining room table should be kept quite simple, but elegant. A few branches of greens encrusted with red glass balls can be placed around large white candles. Put the tallest candle in the middle, graduating the candles to the smallest ones at the ends. Instead of candlesticks use low saucers or place the entire decoration on a mirror. Use a red satin tablecloth if you have one, as it will give "weight" to the room. The finishing touch will be to tie a wreath

Red carnations, evergreen, and interesting pine cones artistically surround five white candles of varying heights which carry out the traditional Christmas colors and glamorize the table. (*Courtesy, Society of American Florists.*)

onto the back of each chair with a large red satin ribbon; this will give the chairs a "dressed for the party" look. Allow the ribbon to be long enough to have streamers hanging down to below the chair seat. Any greens except holly, for holly would stick a passer-by, can be used in these wreaths. Arborvitae would be best.

Storing parts of the tree. Parts of the wall trees can be used again next year. When the holiday season is over, save the cascade streamers and balls, and burn the tree in the back yard. The

Your Dining Room 61

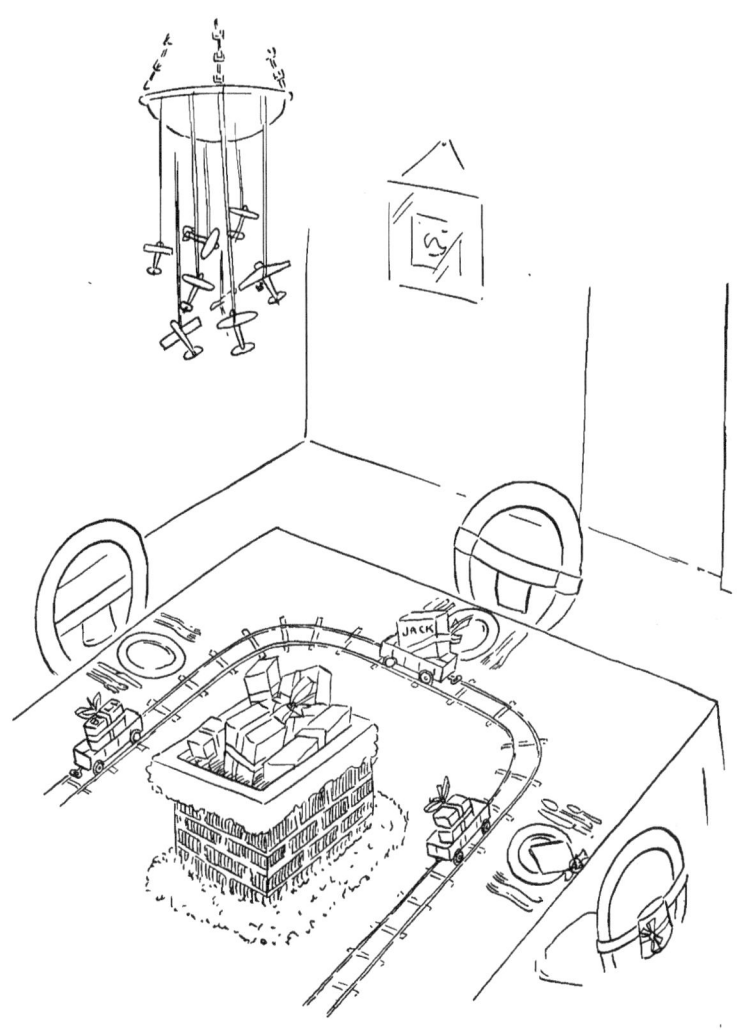

FIGURE 18

branches will burn off, but the wire frame will not be harmed. It can be rolled up in a piece of paper and stored away for another festive season.

CHRISTMAS TABLE FOR BOYS' PARTY

A Christmas table for a boys' party can be made by setting up an electric train on the dining room table (see Figure 18). Use, as a table covering, a cloth that will not be spoiled, or a piece of oilcloth.

If you have some old electric train cars, these can be given a fresh coat of paint for the party. Have a car standing on the tracks at each "plate stop," loaded with a gift for each guest.

A train with an "obstacle" in the center of the table will be more intriguing. A Christmas chimney filled with gifts or favors would be appropriate. This can be made by using any cardboard box, chimney-size, and covering it with red imitation-brick crepe paper. Cotton pasted onto the top and around the bottom will give the desired scenic effect.

Toy airplanes hung on invisible wires from the chandelier will fly around with every gentle breeze.

Red napkins lend a cheery note. Tie a small bell onto one corner of each napkin. Use green yarn to tie it on, and add a few extra loops for color. The bell lends itself to extra conversation. As a "good boy" dividend gift, tie a surprise package onto the back of each chair. A bag of marbles, a few jacks, or a toy airplane are always welcomed by boys. One of these could be opened at the sound of the first napkin bell.

For a package-opening feast of this kind it would be good to have a wastepaper basket tucked under the table to catch the gift wrappings.

Materials. You will need:

- 1 set, new or old, of train tracks
- 1 car in front of each place plate
- 1 small bell for each napkin
- 1 paper chimney
- 6 toy airplanes
- 5 yards of invisible wire
- 1 chair-back gift for each boy
- Gifts for the chimney

Boys always like to be active and this table will keep them very busy and amused, but not too busy to enjoy the dinner.

Christmas Table for Girls' Party

If little girls predominate in your home, they will enjoy a Christmas party using a table set with a dollhouse right in the middle, surrounded by small evergreen trees (see Figure 19).

Your Dining Room 63

Dollhouse. If you do not have a dollhouse, it is easy to make one by taking a cardboard box and covering the sides with red crepe paper having a brick design printed on it. Make windows by pasting on squares of white paper. Draw windowpane lines on with black ink. To provide a roof for the house, tape two pieces of card-

FIGURE 19

board together across the top and then tape to box. Do not worry too much about how far over or down the eaves come, as your cotton snow will cover up any irregularities.

To make a chimney for the house, use a small cardboard box. Cut out a V shape at the bottom so that the box will sit astride the roof of the house. Leave the top of the chimney open, and cover the sides of the chimney with the same red brick crepe paper.

Cover the roof with cotton and sprinkle the entire scene with artificial snow. If you can, put a thin line of cotton on the chimney edge, too, and cover it with snow.

Little trees for around your dollhouse can be made of tiny branches of pine stuck into modeling clay, putty, or wet sand.

Gifts. Put a small, inexpensive gift at each place, wrapped in the gayest paper you can find, and tied with a bright ribbon. Make the bow on the package separate from the actual wrapping ribbon and slip it on with a bobby pin or barrette. The girls will probably want to wear these new bows in their hair right away.

Lollipop favors. Attractive favors can be made out of lollipops. These can also be your place markers. They are very easy to make.

Use two lollipops for each boy or girl candy doll; use one red and one yellow tied together back to back. Cut a piece of picture wire 5" long to make arms. Cut a strip of pink crepe paper 5" long and 1" wide. Twist this around the wire (with the grain of the paper) and fasten it down with gummed tape or glue. Bend the wire in the middle and wrap it once around the sticks, just below the candy "heads."

Bunch up a piece of crepe paper about the size of a dollar bill and pack it around the two sticks for a body. Cut a ½" to ¾" wide strip of red crepe paper. With your finger under the paper on the first turn, wrap up the crushed ball in the movement of a figure 8.

Skirt. For the skirt, cut 30" from a piece of green crepe paper. This makes about four skirts. Now cut against the grain, making 5" wide pieces. Gather the skirt together with your fingers and wrap around the sticks at the waistline, using a piece of string to hold in place. Ruffle out the bottom of the skirt by stretching the paper, being careful not to tear it. Cut features from gummed colored dots and paste them on the lollipops.

Hair. To make hair, take pieces of brown, black, orange, or yellow crepe paper 3" long and 1" wide. Slit them like teeth in a comb. Curl up the ends, as you did for the skirt bottom, for curls of "hair." You can make nice crepe paper curls by pulling the strands of paper gently over a pencil or stick. Paste this on the back lollipop, bringing the ends between the two candies.

Your Dining Room 65

Hat. For the doll hat, make a 2" circle of stiff white paper. Your letter paper would be good for this. Place one of your coffee cups, bottom side down, on the paper and draw around its base. Add some cotton around the edges of the hat, for snow, and paste a bright red bow with four loops at the top for decoration. The hat should be pasted on the top of the lollipop heads.

You might like to give the doll black crepe paper shoes tied with baby ribbon or colored "shoestrings." But if you do not want to make shoes, put your doll's feet in colored gumdrops, which will act as a pedestal or anchor base.

FIGURE 20

Boy doll. Boy candy dolls are just as easy to make. When you fasten the lollipops together, turn the sticks a little apart, so that it will look as though the boy is walking. This also makes it easier to put trousers on his legs. To make his trousers, take two 1" pieces of black crepe paper and paste them around the stick legs. His body will be made the same as for the girl doll, also his arms. His hat likewise will be made the same, except for the crown. For this, crush into a ball a piece of red crepe paper half the size of a dollar bill. Wet it a little and paste a piece of gummed tape from under the edges of the brim across the top, pulling the sides of the hat upward. The boy will need hair and a face, too. Individual workmanship will give all your dolls a lot of originality, once you start making them.

These same candy dolls can be made for parties at other times, by using appropriate color combinations.

Della Robbia Wreath for Mantel

If there is a mantel in your dining room, a colorful Della Robbia wreath (Figure 20) will add much to the feeling of an abundant table. Della Robbia was an Italian artist and goldsmith who worked mostly in clay. He was the first to glaze terra cotta. Many of his designs are still used today, especially at Christmas, for they often represent the Madonna and the Christ Child. Della Robbia's work is readily recognized by the raised white figures superimposed on a clear blue background, the whole being surrounded by colorful wreaths of bright, many-colored fruits or flowers, which frame the sculptured portraits.

Making and decorating the wreath. If you have a light blue plate, this would be an excellent article to build your wreath around. The finished wreath should be shellacked or waxed to make it look like porcelain.

Use plate hooks with wire to hang the plate. Build a wreath on a peat moss base, and fit it over the rim of your dish. Short pine clippings are best for this. There will be no bow on the wreath, but ribbon streamers are permissible if they are yellow or blue, or both. Fasten the wreath onto the plate by wiring through the hanger on the back.

Any of the fruits and berries which do not spoil quickly can be used. Fruit should be put on after it has been tied to wooden picks.

For a flower wreath, use only pastel shades. These can be dipped in paraffin.

A few suggestions for color combinations in fruit: (1) bunches of green grapes and bright kumquats; (2) small oranges with pieces of popcorn stuck in the ends; (3) red apples, polished with wax, arranged with purple grapes.

Two flower combination suggestions: (1) large pink and yellow roses with white poinsettias; (2) pink gardenias and white camellias with yellow mums.

Your Dining Room 67

If you can get shiny leaves to put around each piece of fruit, it will help give the desired porcelain effect.

Wind necklaces of cranberries around the wreath and over the fruit.

Pineapples for candleholders. Instead of using regular candleholders on the mantel, use pineapples (see Figure 20 again). Let the

The religious theme is paramount in this mantel arrangement of evergreen, various-shaped pine cones, berries, religious figurines, and white candles of different heights. (*Courtesy, Society of American Florists.*)

green leaves stay on. Stick a 6" wire into the leaf end of the pineapple. Bend the leaves of the pineapple open with your left hand, being careful not to break them. Have the candle near your right hand and ready for use. Heat the wire over a flame. When the wire is hot, stick it through the center of the candle. Hold until set.

Tie blue ribbon around the green pineapple spikes, forming some jaunty streamers with knots in the ends. Construct a pair of these pineapples and use blue-and-white saucers as bases on the mantel.

Materials. You will need:

>   1 blue plate, or a blue-and-white willowware dinner plate
>   1 set of plate hooks with wire hanger
>   Fruit or flowers
>   1 basic wreath padded with peat moss (you can get one at a florist's shop)
>   1 long necklace of cranberries for the fruit
>   Leis of tiny white flowers, for the flower wreath
>   2 yards of ¾" blue grosgrain ribbon
>   2 blue candles
>   2 blue-and-white saucers

Glorified Della Robbia wreath. A glorified Della Robbia wreath can be made of pine branches painted a light blue, using imitation or real fruit which has been gilded. With this you will not need a porcelain plate in the center. Use blue candles in gold or gilded candlesticks. Coffee tins painted with gold and tied with a blue ribbon are effective. Fill the cans with wet sand or earth and the candle will stay straighter.

For an added touch to your fireplace, throw cinnamon and cloves on your fire to give it a gourmet fragrance.

Door to Kitchen or Pantry

On the door which leads to the kitchen or pantry, make a life-sized Santa Claus out of red oilcloth or cardboard, or buy one already made (see Figure 19 again).

Stovepipe candy canes. Put the largest candy canes in town by the side of your Santa Claus—one on either side of the door (see Figure 19). These can be made out of stovepipes painted white or wrapped with white paper and trimmed with red ribbons or red cellophane tape wound around them. These colored canes can be stored away and used next year—perhaps at your front entrance.

You will need for one gigantic candy cane:

>   2 sections of regular 24" stovepipe
>   1 elbow of stovepipe
>   1 small can of white enamel
>   6 yards of red satin ribbon 1" wide

Your Kitchen 69

Assemble the two pieces of straight stovepipe. Place upright on a piece of paper and paint them, leaving the joining half-inch at the top unpainted. Paint the elbow inside and out. Join together when thoroughly dry.

With your ribbon, start at the mouth of the elbow and fasten one end of the ribbon to the inside of the pipe with heavy gummed white tape. Start wrapping around the joint, then downward in a curving direction until you reach the bottom. Tape the ribbon well to the inside of the pipe at the bottom. Tape it in several places across the rear so that the ribbon will stay in place. A dot of glue may do the trick.

FIGURE 21

YOUR KITCHEN

Your kitchen will be so filled with Christmas goodies there will not be much space left for decoration. But something can be done for the cupboard and windows.

Cupboard. The inside of your cupboard doors can be made gay with red paper Santa Clauses or colored pictures of food and recipes cut from magazines—such as a beautiful turkey sitting on a table by a bowl of cranberry sauce or red Jell-O salad molds tied with white ribbons of whipped cream. Paper holly wreaths can be thumbtacked on the outside of the doors for easy removal later. Give your cupboard a holiday air by putting on the shelves some crepe paper edging decorated with Christmas designs.

Windows. You will want your windows to look cozy inside and still to be filled with sunlight. Two or three four-inch-wide bands of white crepe paper, slit like a comb, and cut curve-fashion in the form of a Christmas tree across your window, can be very effective (see Figure 21). Place a star at the center top. You can thumbtack a band of holly paper around the woodwork of your window and still have plenty of light.

Along your kitchen window you can make decorative flowerpot holders by taking old tin cans and painting them white. Spiral some red gummed tape down the side, candy cane fashion. Fill with sand or cinders and add a small pine branch or two with a pine cone in the center. These will look inviting to the passer-by.

If the children eat breakfast in the kitchen, use a Christmas design crepe paper tablecloth and cover with thin white plastic, or paste pictures on their table mats with Scotch tape. These can be removed later.

Now that your kitchen is all dressed up, why not stay in it and make some popcorn balls? Popcorn balls are always in demand at Christmas time.

Popcorn Balls

To make popcorn balls, mix 2 cups of sugar and ½ cup of dark syrup in 1¼ cups of hot water. Cook slowly, without stirring, to 260° F., until the candy forms a firm ball. Now add 1 teaspoon of vanilla, 1 tablespoon of vinegar, and ½ teaspoon of salt. Recook to 260° F. or until a solid but not brittle ball is formed in cold water. While the syrup is cooking refreshen 5 quarts of popped corn in the oven. Keep hot. When the syrup is ready remove the corn from the oven. Pour the syrup lightly over the popcorn and stir gently with a wooden spoon. Use a litle vegetable oil on your hands, cupping the popcorn into balls. Wrap each ball in cellophane and tie with a bright ribbon. In the South, where pecans are grown, they like to sprinkle 2 cups of these chopped nut meats on the popcorn and mix them in before adding syrup. Walnuts or roasted peanuts could also be used.

The syrup can be tinted with any of your kitchen vegetable

Your Library 71

colorings. Pale green or red are most attractive. These balls make lovely tree decorations, especially when wrapped in clear cellophane.

For a special popcorn ball, form it over a lollipop and paint the wooden handle green. Tie with a red ribbon bow. Stick the wooden handle into an apple (see Figure 22). Use as a table decoration. These are good to hang on the Christmas tree, too. Best of all, the children know popcorn balls are to be eaten.

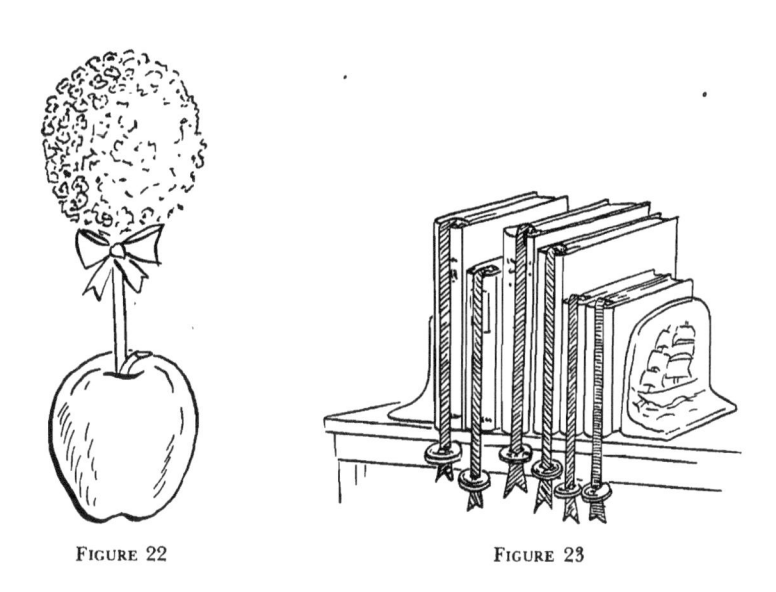

FIGURE 22

FIGURE 23

YOUR LIBRARY

Book markers. Add a decorative note to your library by using red, green, and white ribbon book markers (Figure 23). Make them of 1½" wide grosgrain ribbon in colors of red and green, and some white for "accent." Cut the ribbons the length of the average book height in your library and add 4" or more (2" for the inside of the book, a certain amount to hang down over the edge of the shelf, and 1" for the knot).

Place the markers in the backs of the books so that the ribbons hang over and down the outside. Enough of the title will show for the bookworm to be able to find what he wants. As the books are uneven in height, the single-length markers, falling irregularly down the backs of the books, provide an extra point of interest for your room.

Tie a knot in the ends of the ribbons to weight them down. A more decorative finish is to slide Chinese coins over the ends. (The New York, Boston, Chicago, and San Francisco Chinatowns sell these pennies by the string or by the piece.) These coins will make good weights for the ends of your ribbons.

FIGURE 24

Basket or bird cage for Christmas greens. In the library doorway or from the chandelier, hang a wire bird cage or basket of Christmas greens with red and white carnations tucked under the branches. In the bird cage it is easy to have a small bowl of water for the thirsty flowers. In the basket, however, you will need druggist's test tubes filled with water-soaked cotton for their stems.

Bookcase. If your books are in a case with glass doors, open the doors wide—if they will not be in the way—and garland with smilax over the top and down their keyhole sides. Tack four red paper balls

Your Music Room 73

on the top of the door, above the hinge sides and at each front corner. (See Figure 24.)

Add a cranberry desk tree to an inside shelf. Make the tree by stringing cranberries on wire and bending the wires to form branches. Stick these in moist sand encrusted with snow. Snow can be made with heavy soapsuds powdered with artificial snowflakes.

FIGURE 25

YOUR MUSIC ROOM

CHRISTMAS MUSIC BOX

How about a Christmas Music Box (Figure 25) for your music room?

Take a bureau drawer and line it with red cardboard (a desk blotter or two will do for this).

Lay the drawer on edge, lengthwise, on a table or piano, handle side up. Set little musical figures inside. Stick thumbtacks 1" apart down the sides of the drawer and tightly stretch gold wrapping string back and forth across the front to form the lines, or staff, for notes.

Select a favorite carol and count the notes in the first two bars of music. Make your "notes" of black grosgrain baby ribbon. Count the number of notes you will need, and cut the ribbon into 4" pieces. Fold the top ½" of each note L-shaped, and sew with black thread. Cut the remainder of the ribbon into 3" pieces to make the desired number of tailored bows. To make the bow, fold the ribbon back and forth like an S and shirr through the center with your fingers. Now bring the end of the note over the center of the bow for a knot, and stitch at the back. Cut a tiny 1" snowball out of plastic foam. Pin the snowball behind the bow by sticking long pins through the knot and into the ball. Make as many notes as you will need for the two bars of music which you have selected.

Have the children follow the music and tie the notes on the gold strings at their proper places.

Encircle the drawer with a pine garland.

Place tall white candles at each side of your music box. For candlesticks, use gold-painted coffee cans. Fill them with sand encrusted with red glass beads.

Carry out the gold theme in your room by sewing gold glass balls along the edges of your window drapes.

YOUR BEDROOMS

Add a festive air to the bedrooms in your home.

On the outside of the door. A decoration on the outside of each door will personalize the Christmas spirit. A color scheme contrasting with or matching the hall or doors should be consistently carried out, with gold, silver and red, red and white, or red and green predominating. Our example will be for gold and blue.

On the master bedroom door you could hang a gold wreath tied with a lovely light blue satin ribbon.

Grandmother's door could have an old-fashioned bouquet made of straw flowers backed by a gold paper doily. This could be tied with a florist's sheer ribbon of the color on her walls.

For the baby's door use bright-colored balloons, one blue, tied with a gold ribbon. This decoration will amuse the child.

Your Bedrooms 75

A teen girl might enjoy candy canes held in place with small blue bows ending in many streamers. On the end of each streamer tie, in the form of cake favors, miniature dancing slippers, skates, footballs, and the like. These should be dipped in gold paint. The canes are not real candy, but are made by wrapping white and red crepe paper around some of grandfather's walking sticks.

A boy might like a pair of mitts cut out of cardboard, painted gold, and hung on the door with blue ribbons.

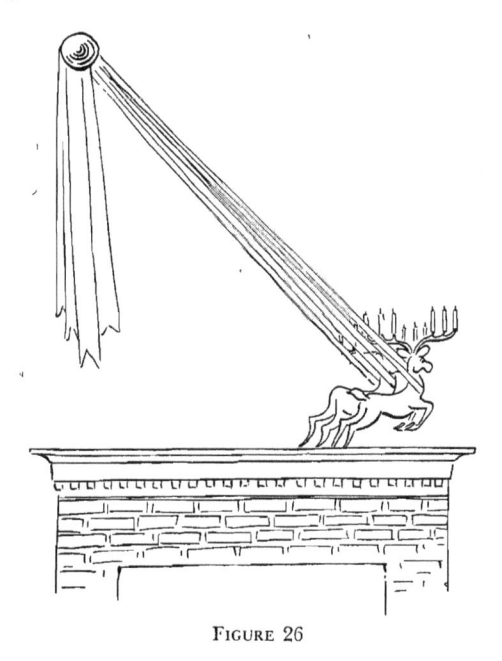

FIGURE 26

Inside the room. Inside the master bedroom silver stars hanging on invisible wires against one wall would be chic. On the dressing table a pair of pastel or white Christmas trees, such as those in the powder room, would be appropriate. Tie a large ribbon on one corner of the dressing table or around the chair. If you have a mantel, father might like to see a pair of reindeer with a tiny candle on each antler, and a small wreath around the neck of each animal. Long red streamer "reins" could be tacked over the mantel. (See Figure 26.)

Grandmother might like her curtains tied back with Christmas ribbons, and a big bow on her bedpost. On her mantel put a tree of dried branches painted white and tied with a red ribbon taped high above the mantel.

The baby will love his own Christmas tree in his room. Place it in the play pen so that he will not get scratched or knock the tree

A jolly Santa Claus with reindeer entirely of white can welcome the guests from the front lawn. Build the scene on wooden crates covered with white oilcloth. The figures are of papier-mâché painted white, with cotton for Santa's beard. The tall white candles are made from mailing tubes. Evergreen branches form background. (*Courtesy of Lewis D. Moorhead.*)

over. Bright-colored balloons make a good decoration for the baby's tree.

YOUR YARD

On the trees in your yard why not hang food cups for the birds? These can be made by taking half a grapefruit hull and forming a basket. Fill the hull with suet and grain. Add a bit of Christmas

Your Yard

greens and tie on a tree branch with bright red and green ribbon, or with shoestrings dyed in various colors.

Your front porch can be made to join the holiday spirit by adding red and green gourds weatherproofed with varnish and tied to the rail posts or hanging from eave corners.

Out-of-doors Christmas tree. If you have a pine tree in your yard, why not share it with your community as an out-of-doors Christmas tree?

The tree can be decorated with all the tin and copper kitchen pans you can spare or can borrow from your neighbors. Various shapes and molds are effective, such as hearts, fish, and stars. The large star at the top should be a star mold.

During the year save the round tops and bottoms of your food tins. These are lovely hanging from the yard tree branches. Apples and oranges hung on the tree are bright accents of color and they will keep well out of doors if your climate is mild.

For highlights on the tree hang bunches of nails which have been dipped in gold paint.

For the living tree, buy specially made electric wires for out of doors. Your local store will advise you. Spot floodlights can be turned on at night. Blue bulbs seem to give the best effect.

Drape any kind of berried branches over the tree, such as mistletoe, bay, or holly. Ropes of cranberries and popcorn are always enjoyed by the birds and they make colorful decorations.

WARNING. Every precaution should be taken to prevent fires and accidents. Make certain that all decorating materials are fireproofed, that lighted candles are protected, open fireplaces screened, and ash trays adequate. Remove small throw rugs, provide light on steps, avoid overcrowding. Think always of *safety first*.

3

SPECIAL OCCASIONS

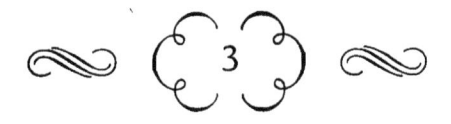

SPECIAL OCCASIONS

*D*ECORATING for traditional holidays is lots of fun, but decorating for personal affairs is a joy and well worth your time and talent. Decorations help make birthdays happy, showers gay, weddings memorable; club meetings important, church services impressive. Start with flowers or table decorations, then add as much more as imagination and time will allow.

CHILDREN'S PARTIES

Children's parties in particular are a challenge—you must capture the interest of the child or your decorative scheme is a failure.

FLORAL ARRANGEMENTS

Children's parties can be held at any time of the year, generally in celebration of their birthdays. The following floral arrangements would be suitable for a children's party.

A lollipop tree can be made by arranging long-stemmed chrysanthemums in a radiating design so that lollipops may be tied to the stems to look like fruit on a tree.

In a round container, arrange daisies, daffodils, or petunias, depending on the season. Include, in your arrangement, a branching shrub such as pussy willow, with little dolls sitting on the branches.

A merry-go-round can be made from a round container, such as an angel food tin, by covering it with paper and paper decorations of horses, poles, and so on. Candy canes to resemble poles can be attached with transparent tape. Seasonal flowers may be placed in the tube of the container.

For boys, have an "Out on the Range" party. Arrange flowers, perhaps marigolds and zinnias, in an imitation cowboy hat, which may be a round bowl covered with brown crepe paper. Place an imitation cowboy and cowgirl on horse figurines around the hat. To carry out your color scheme, use a yellow or brown tablecloth, and serve chocolate ice cream with cookies cut into the shape of horses' heads.

In a "Surrey with the Fringe on Top" container, use mixed spring flowers in the spring, or asters or pompons in the fall.

For a November birthday. For a November birthday, for which the chrysanthemum is the flower of the month and yellow topaz is the birthstone, individual yellow pompon nosegays can be arranged around the base of citrus-iced angel food cake on which there are yellow birthday candles. The tablecloth might be yellow or white with round amber disks attached here and there to resemble topaz stones. Use either white or gold tapers to which gold sequins have been attached.

Another suggestion for a child's birthday party is to arrange chrysanthemums in a low container. Make faces on mum heads with cloves and cinnamon candies or gumdrops. Put bow ties and lace doily collars on flower stems under the flowers. Make little gumdrop dolls for place cards by using toothpicks and small gumdrops. Sometimes Life Saver candies are used, too.

Circus Party

A circus party lends itself to a host of decorative ideas. For instance, you may use a clown as a centerpiece. Take a piece of cardboard the desired width and roll it into a cylinder. Fasten this with Scotch tape. Paste simple features made of different-colored paper on both front and back; perhaps one side can be grumpy, the other laughing. Make a clown hat of green crepe paper with yellow dots pasted on it and surround the face with a gathered piece of yellow

The Wedding

crepe paper for the clown's collar. From the chandelier above, hang different circus animals made of cardboard. In the center of this hanging group you might show a man on a flying trapeze. Favors can consist of gay-colored hats and of baskets to which a small full-length clown is attached. In his hand is a card on which the child's name is written.

BRIDAL SHOWERS

Bridal shower decorations should be dainty and feminine to echo the loveliness of the prospective bride.

The crepe paper umbrella has become a tradition for showers. (Use the frame of a real umbrella for this.) Place the umbrella at the back of a gift table decorated with crepe paper and arrange the gifts so that they appear to be spilling out of it.

A clever table decoration would be to suspend a green crepe-paper-covered watering can (in a pouring position) from the ceiling. From the spout, hang ribbon streamers at the ends of which are tied small items suggesting the kind of shower you are having.

A cupid in the center of the table could be holding in his hands hearts on which the initials of the engaged couple have been printed in gold. Surround the cupid with tiny corsages, one for each guest.

Flowers are a lovely tribute to the bride-to-be. Decorate with flowers the ribs of a small parasol. Tie to the handle a corsage for the bride.

Amidst a mound of flower boutonnieres for guests, stand large paper engagement and wedding rings. The bride's corsage will be tied to the top of the engagement ring.

Another setting for a floral arrangement would be to use figures of the bride and groom in the center, with seasonal flowers around them.

THE WEDDING

The floral arrangements for a wedding should be as lovely as you can possibly afford. This is a special day to be remembered always.

Cake and Floral Centerpieces at Reception

At the wedding reception, the cake and floral centerpiece or twin floral arrangements should be unified. The floral table decorations should not overpower the wedding cake nor detract from it. Often a spray of real flowers or a miniature of the bride's bouquet is placed on the top of the cake. Miniature figures of a bride and groom standing under a flowery bower may be perched atop the cake. Flowers may also circle the base of the cake and perhaps link the two floral arrangements.

Although white flowers are traditional at wedding receptions, modern brides often prefer pastel tints to offset the white cake and tablecloth. Pink, especially, is a popular color for wedding reception flowers. However, if colored flowers are used, they must harmonize with the room color scheme.

When a center table and smaller tables in a public dining room are used for large wedding receptions, each table should have a floral centerpiece.

SILVER WEDDING ANNIVERSARY

For your silver wedding anniversary, bring out as much of the silver idea in your decorations as possible. Decorations can consist of small silver bells arranged in garlands over doorways. Large silver leaves in white bowls can be placed here and there around the room.

Menu. If you are planning to have a buffet supper, the following menu would carry out your silver-and-white theme.

Consommé
White fish on a silver platter
White potatoes
Chicken salad in a silver bowl
Iced tea in clear glasses
Angel food cake

Floral arrangements for table. Here are suggestions for floral arrangements that will add charm to your table.

Twin arrangements of white roses and silvered eucalyptus leaves can be fixed in a silver sugar and creamer.

Golden Wedding Anniversary 85

White snapdragons and roses can be arranged in a silver bun warmer or in another silver utensil.

Place white spray orchids and variegated ivy in a silver rectangular container.

Twine lilies of the valley or other white flowers around a large tin-foil-covered "wedding band" placed vertically in a low container.

Gardenias or other flowers can float at the base.

GOLDEN WEDDING ANNIVERSARY

The olden days. For your golden wedding anniversary ask your guests to come in old-fashioned clothes. Have as many of your original wedding party present as possible.

Get out your wedding dress and (try to) have it fitted to you for the occasion. Ask each guest to bring his or her photograph.

During the party ask your guests to sign their names and addresses on a wall or screen or in a book and paste their pictures alongside their signatures. This will go down in family history. After all the guests have arrived, have one of them play the wedding march for your entrance. During the evening you will enjoy singing songs which were popular fifty years ago.

Buffet supper. Golden food for your buffet supper:

>Hard-boiled egg yolks in consommé
>Roast turkey with saffron rice
>Carrot salad and baked sweet potatoes
>Ambrosia, made mostly of sliced oranges, with orange sherbet
>Golden wedding cake (recipe in most cookbooks)
>Hot tea and hot coffee

Flower arrangements. Here are some flower arrangement suggestions for a golden wedding anniversary.

Fill any beautiful container with yellow roses and gilded leaves.

The "wedding band" suggestion under "Silver Wedding Anniversary" may be used, but cover the band with gold paper.

Use a gilt manzanita tree in the middle of the table and trim it with white Phalaenopsis or purple baby orchids.

Yellow and bronze chrysanthemums with gilt foliage in a bronze container would be appropriate.

BABY SHOWERS

A baby shower is a friendly way to provide gifts of clothing and other necessities for "the most wonderful baby in all the world." A little book entitled *So You're Expecting a Baby*, available without cost from the U. S. Children's Bureau, Washington 25, D. C., will make a nice gift for "mother." This book lists the items required for baby's wardrobe, and gift items selected from this list will prove useful and appropriate.

Decorations. This is a "sitting party" and home decorations should be above eye level, such as streamers from the chandelier to the corners of the room, or to picture frames.

Flower arrangements. Flower arrangement suggestions for the baby shower include the following: (1) Twin baby bootie arrangements, one with pink and one with blue flowers. (2) A baby crib container with a doll in it with flowers encircling the base. (3) A plastic tree with baby booties and other baby garments in the middle of the table; twin flower arrangements on either side.

Another table centerpiece idea is to decorate a doll bassinet with pastel ribbon and place the shower gifts inside.

A baby doll, appropriately dressed and holding a small bouquet of flowers, makes another novel centerpiece.

Make a cardboard stork for your centerpiece. In his bill can be a diaper in which a baby doll is supported. Surround this with tiny corsages for each guest.

PROMS

Decorating the Gymnasium or Ballroom

An effective way to decorate your gymnasium or ballroom for a prom, at very little expense, is to make long 1½" wide streamers of heavy paper (not cardboard). Paste gold foil on one side and tin or aluminum foil on the other. These can be bought for very little money. Make other sets of streamers using your school colors, one on each side.

Tie a rope on the end of each streamer and fasten one end securely to the wall. Take the other end and start twisting the rope until it is as tight as you can get it. Now secure the end you are twisting to the center light or ceiling of your room. The twisting will make the streamers twirl all evening.

Walls and doorways and windows. For the walls and around doorways and windows get the tops and bottoms of as many round tin cans as you can collect. The one-gallon-tin size is very good for this purpose. Wash the lids and bottoms so that there is no food smell to the metal. Avoid fish can lids.

Cut pictures of flowers from magazines, shape round, and paste in the center of the lid. Hang these medallions around the doors and windows. For hangers, punch a hole with a nail and hammer and tie satin baby ribbon, in your school colors, through the holes. Hang some of these pictures on invisible wires from the center where the colored ropes meet. They will turn and flicker all evening.

You will be surprised at how handsome your old gymnasium will look.

Before orchestra platform. Two large gold (painted paper) cornucopias filled with flowers will show up well in front of the orchestra platform.

YOUR CHURCH AND CLUB

YOUR CHURCH AND CLUB

SHOWERS, weddings, and anniversaries are all joyous occasions for which you are free to use any suitable decorative idea you may have. There are, however, times when you find it necessary to serve on a decorating committee.

YOUR CHURCH

FLOWER ARRANGEMENTS

If you are a member of a flower committee for the church, you should keep in mind that pastel-colored flowers are best for church arrangements, since they impart a feeling of dignity and reverence.

Take the flower arrangements to church early enough to give yourself time to rearrange them should that be necessary. If possible sit in the rear of the church and look carefully at your handiwork. Aside from the altar, a few well-done arrangements are better than a lot of flowers which have been placed at odd intervals. As the chancel is a focal point of interest, an arrangement in front or on either side is pleasing (see Figure 27).

Put a bowl of bright-colored flowers in your church entrance to give a welcome greeting.

FLOWER CALENDAR

This calendar may have suggestions for your flower committee. Find the branches, flowers, and vegetables in your own garden.

FIGURE 27

January: Arrangement of branches and leaves painted white, in a white bowl.
February: Natural branches and forced bulb flowers.
March: Forced spring branches of forsythia or cherry.
April: Fruit tree branches and any bulb flowers.
May: Flowered branches and iris; tulips with roses.
June: White peonies with candy tuft.
July: Roses with delphinium.
August: Pompon and large asters, with polished leaves.
September: Chrysanthemums of various sizes, all one color.
October: Autumn leaves and dried grasses such as grain heads, burrs, and vegetable pods.
November: Corn and pumpkins.
December: Any of the evergreens used indoors; Christmas roses are a must.

For special Sundays such as Palm Sunday, palm leaves are most important. For Easter you will want white lilies and dogwood.

Also see the spring flower arrangement suggestions in this book.

YOUR CLUB

Spring Flower Arrangements

Here are some spring flower arrangements which could be used as helpful suggestions by women's organizations such as Parent-Teacher Associations, Federated Women's Clubs, garden clubs, Women's Farm Councils, church auxiliaries, home demonstration clubs, Future Homemakers of America, women's auxiliaries of veterans associations.

Entrance hall. The entrance hall should be alive with green floral decorations. On the mantel have a large arrangement of iris in lovely orchid shades, enhanced by brass and crystal candelabra. By the door a small bowl of pink rose buds, lily of the valley, and white candy tuft could greet the guests. On a table against one wall put a contrasting square turquoise bowl with purple iris. On another table put a bowl of deep pink beauty bush branches. High in one corner place an unusual bowl filled with red and purple tulips, with their large leaves held up by natural tree branches. In the foyer have a large arrangement of yellow iris with their spiked leaves towering over yellow pansies, and any other small yellow flowers, such as riniculum with arborvitae, filling in the background.

Speakers' room. The main speakers' room may be decorated with an arrangement of pale old-fashioned roses in a silver bowl, forming a high vine design. On top of a table or buffet, an all-white arrangement could be used with long branches of snowballs in a dark crystal vase flanked by white candles.

President's table. On the speakers' or president's table place a small cut-crystal bowl of tea roses. Flank this table with the American flag on one side and the Club's flag on the other.

If a Meal Is Served

Dining room. If a meal is to be served in connection with the meeting, special attention should be given to the flowers in the dining room. The dining room mantel could have an enormous arrangement of iris and dogwood, with large polished leaves filling in the background. If there is another mantel or buffet in the room, decorate it with an arrangement of deep-red roses and matching red tulips in a square dish heightened by pine boughs.

Hall leading to dining room. In the hall leading to the dining room make a grouping of white narcissus, snowballs, and white iris arranged in a blue bowl. Somewhere a large arrangement of long Scotch broom or forsythia would be lovely in a green bowl. If these are not to be had, you will, of course, have to choose other flowers that are seasonal.

Speakers' table. At the speakers' table you might use a beautiful all-pink arrangement of roses, tulips, and beauty branches. Farther down the table put a bowl of purple iris and pink beauty branches. On the other side of the speakers' place, still farther down the table, put a bowl of white dogwood, yellow roses, purple iris, and white snowdrops.

Center and side tables. On a center table a blue bowl could hold white narcissus and yellow daffodils. A side table could have a vase of pink and white branches; another table, white and purple iris with large beauty branches in a white bowl. A bowl of white narcissus and purple iris could greet the guests as they enter the dining room.

5

FLOWER AND TABLE ARRANGEMENTS

FLOWER AND TABLE ARRANGEMENTS

AN ARTISTIC flower arrangement conveys so much more beauty and joy than a bouquet carelessly stuck into a vase. Creating an artistic arrangement is an art, but not too difficult a one for an amateur to master. Apply the basic principles of design, add a little imagination, and you will have a beautiful arrangement.

THREE KINDS OF ARRANGEMENTS

There are three types of arrangements: Modern, including line, crescent, and curving arrangements; Traditional, including massed and Colonial arrangements; and Oriental or Symbolical arrangements. (In the latter, the highest leaves or flowers symbolize heaven, the middle height represents man, and the lowest line is for earth.)

Flowers with curving stems, such as petunias, daisies, sweet peas, and Tritomas, are excellent for crescent and curving arrangements. The straighter-stemmed flowers, such as carnations and chrysanthemums, are used most effectively in line and Oriental arrangements. Dominant flowers, such as chrysanthemums, dahlias and peonies, are suggested for massed arrangements. Delicate flowers, such as delphiniums and sweetheart or garnet roses, are ideal for Colonial arrangements.

Amateurs usually want to learn how to create triangular arrangements. For this design, the longest stem should be one and one-half to two times the height or width of the container. Insert the backbone of the design first, then fill in with the shorter-stemmed flowers on the sides. No two stems should be the same length. The largest and darkest flowers are used for the base of the design and the center of interest. The buds and smallest flowers are for the outermost points of the design.

The completed arrangement should have all the essentials of good design: unity of lines, proper proportion, balance, color harmony, and a center of interest.

Working materials. For any of the arrangements, you will need various working materials, for it is very difficult to achieve the proper appearance without some basic supplies. You should have a suitable container, scissors, a knife, a stem holder (needle holder, frog, or small-mesh chicken wire), putty or suction cups (to keep stem holder stationary if flowers are heavy), thin wire, and wire clippers.

PRECAUTIONS TO BE OBSERVED

Fragrances and colors. Do not mix too many fragrances in a bouquet. For instance, roses, gardenias, and carnations all have lovely fragrances of their own and so should be used alone. Do not use too many colors in one arrangement; two or three should be the limit, and remember to group your colors instead of spotting them throughout your arrangement.

Leaves and stems. There should be no crossing of leaves or stems. Each leaf, stem, and flower plays a definite role in the design. If the flowers you are using do not have distinctive foliage of their own, use other leaves—such as croton, sansevieria, dranaena, magnolia, caladium, or evergreen. Never crowd too many flowers and leaves into a vase, as this bruises the stems and makes the arrangement less artistic.

All stems should be cut diagonally to help them absorb the most water. The leaves must be removed below the water level so that they will not decay and foul the water. Some flower stems need special treatment. Milky or gummy stems—such as those of poinsettias, dahlias, and hydrangeas—should have their stems seared, immediately upon cutting, or quickly dipped into boiling water for a few

Table Arrangements from Your Vegetable Garden 99

seconds. The hairy stems of zinnias and poppies should be singed slightly. Thick stems, such as those of chrysanthemums and Easter lilies, should be slit a little. Some people thoughtlessly break or snap chrysanthemum stems instead of cutting them. You will be surprised how much proper treatment of stems prolongs the beauty of an arrangement.

Making flowers last. By using one of the commercial preparations in the water to lengthen the life of the flowers, you will avoid changing the water every day. As soon as the lower blossoms of spike flowers—gladioli, delphiniums, snapdragons, stock, and the like—become wilted, they should be removed, the stems shortened, and the arrangement kept unified. Never place an arrangement in a sunny window, in a draft, on a mantel over a burning fireplace, or near a radiator, if you want it to last well.

Adding interest. Your arrangements will be more interesting if you use figurines, leaves, fruit, or gourds to suggest the spirit of the season or to portray a mood or theme.

TABLE ARRANGEMENTS FROM YOUR VEGETABLE GARDEN

In late spring and summer as well as early fall a centerpiece of vegetables fresh from your garden makes an unusual arrangement. If you do not have a garden, pick up a few fresh vegetables at your grocer's—green peppers, tomatoes, some of the curly Chinese cabbage, red cabbage, carrots, mushrooms, or any vegetable in season which has a beautiful shape and color.

With the mushrooms, an arrangement of moss or an upside-down pie pan with little gnomes or woods figures will add a cool touch. In the center of the pie pan place, flat side down, a large potato which has been cut in two pieces. Cut twigs from a pine tree or arborvitae will make a forest in the middle. This is very cool-looking, especially if placed on a mirror. The potato will keep the pine fresh. (A potato is also excellent for keeping greens fresh in a Christmas crèche.)

Provide yourself with a porcelain figure such as a little girl, a little boy, or a water nymph. Surround the figure with fresh vegetables, putting a few of the smaller ones in the figure's arms. Try to get a realistic effect.

If you have a porcelain frog, let him sit on a mirror with string beans, for seaweed, scattered over it. Add one or two tomatoes with a white flower stuck in the stem end.

Flower arrangements for outdoor table. Here are a few flower arrangement suggestions for an outdoor table setting.

Fill a green pottery container with red and yellow flowers, such as zinnias, Peruvian lilies, and snapdragons. Use plaid place mats or a plaid tablecloth.

Work up a South Sea Islands theme. Place bird-of-paradise flowers with tropical foliage in a wooden bowl. Straw place mats would add a final touch.

Place mats or a tablecloth of eyelet embroidery would look pretty on a table placed on a terrace or outside the house. In the center arrange peach tuberose, begonias, or pink rubrum lilies in a low arrangement. Use white caladium leaves for foliage accent.

6

DECORATING FOR PROFIT

DECORATING FOR PROFIT

THE SPIRIT of any one of the American holidays is made gay and festive by the use of any of the appropriate decorations described in this book. But a certain amount of artistic skill and aptitude is required to create or arrange them, and while most people have such creative ability, many for lack of time, space, or materials are unable to do the work.

For these reasons a ready market exists for the sale of really artistic decorations. You can earn money by supplying this market with items made in your home; or by gathering materials such as evergreens, seed pods, shells, flowers, and the like and selling them direct to florists or other individuals.

Another money-making opportunity awaits the person who has a flair for arranging displays. If you have this flair, plus the physical requirements of health and agility, you might decorate halls, church bazaar booths, fraternity dance rooms, and even store display windows.

Table decorations and floral arrangements require a special type of artistry—that of understanding color, line, and balance. You'll find a market for this type of service at weddings, parties, and club meetings, in doctors' offices, and perhaps even in churches.

If you have the ability to teach others how to decorate, you can earn money as a guest lecturer before women's groups.

For a fee you might conduct a class at a YWCA, or for a Scout group or similar groups. To approach in a sensible way the many opportunities for making money in this field, a few points need special consideration:

Possibilities of success. First survey the market for probable sales to determine the volume of business you might be able to build up. Also consider the type of competition.

Personal qualifications. Appraise your own talent and resources honestly. You'll need health, energy, and time, plus the ability to organize and manage. You must have integrity and a sense of responsibility. If you sell direct to consumers, you'll need a friendly personality. If you must remain at home, you'll need to employ someone who can go out and sell for you.

Product. Make a definite decision as to what you want to sell, so that you can build a sound business as you develop. The product should be salable and uniform, have eye appeal, and give the satisfaction the customer has a right to expect. Decide where and how it is to be sold—mail order, road stand, house to house, stores, florists, and so on.

Production. Be prepared for large orders. Many people can sell a few items, but if a big order comes in they find themselves unable to cope with the situation. To avoid this, have a backlog of supplies, have ready sources for more if you need them in a hurry, and have friends or helpers on whom you can call in such an emergency.

Learn to streamline your operations so that you can accomplish the most with the least cost and effort. Timing is important. Have items ready ahead of the season so that delivery can be made on the dot!

Package. Nearly every type of merchandise needs some type of package to protect it, to display it, or to deliver it, or for storing it on shelves. And the cost of such a package must be included in the price of the item.

Profit. No one can stay long in any business without making a profit. Without profit there is no incentive. Figure your costs honestly. Consider time spent in gathering material, time spent in making or assembling the items, time spent in designing or arranging, and time spent in delivery. Also include overhead (room, light, phone, and heat), supplies and upkeep and replacement—and of course taxes!

Perseverance. It takes time to get established in any kind of business—time to learn all the short cuts, time to establish good business contacts, and time to gain a good reputation for reliability.

Don't give up easily. Stick to your job and keep an eye open for profitable side lines. If the business is strictly a Christmas item like wreaths or trees, you may be able to branch out with an item for birthdays, weddings, or some such related field.

Enthusiasm, alertness, and a belief in yourself are necessary to help you get started in any business.

HOW TO GET STARTED

Introduce your product or your artistic skill before a group such as a woman's club, church, or school group.

Do a decorating job for some charity affair without cost but with recognition on the program.

Take samples to buyers in stores, shops, or market places.

Place items on consignment at roadside stands, in tourist shops, or in stores.

Advertise in your local paper.

Write a note or send a sample by mail to prospective buyers.

Give lectures before groups and let them know you are in business.

Watch the papers and the society columns for coming events; then contact the person in charge and ask for the job of decorating.

TWENTY-FOUR IDEAS FOR ITEMS TO SELL

Idea 1: Wreaths. Go around to your neighbors and friends and take orders for Christmas wreaths and other decorations which you can make for a few pennies. These also make nice gifts, saving you money and yet making a very welcome addition to a friend's house at Christmas.

In the early fall gather milkweed pods, pompons, sea shells, and driftwood at the seashore. Gather cat-o'-nine-tails, leaves, stems, small pine branches, cones and any attractive dried flowers and seed pods, and small logs about 12 to 15 inches long and several inches in diameter. Gather anything which grows in the woods but is not poisonous. Bring these home and hang them to dry in a place where they won't clutter up the house. Around the end of November go about trimming the uneven branches of the evergreen trees in

FIGURE 28

your neighborhood; be sure to ask your friends which branches to trim. You might also gather them from your own or your friends' woods. Get yourself a work table which will be out of the way of the family, for your sake and theirs.

To make a wreath (Figure 28): Gild the cones, long grass, and pods. Silver the leaves. This can be done with inexpensive radiator paint. Hang to dry.

Equipment you will need: a supply of evergreens and holly, florist's wire, paper plates, clothesline wire, peat moss or dried grass, picture wire, ribbon (red, green, and white), lacquer (red, green, and blue), gold and silver paint, red berries, and a ball of green string.

Cut out the center of the paper plate; pad the plate rim with peat moss or dried grass and wrap with string. This gives you a doughnut effect, only flatter. You can make a wire frame of any desired size if you do not want to use paper plates. Attach a hanger to the back,

Twenty-four Ideas for Items to Sell

using picture wire, or reshape a wire coat hanger, leaving the hook in place. Hang the wreath on the wall or work with it flat on a table.

Place the evergreens on the circle, holding the stems in your left hand. Have the needles pointing up. Place the evergreens with the first bunch parallel to the circle, slanting them a little to the left. Your next bunch goes directly below, pointing a little to the right, and so on around. Wrap or tie the branches on with spool wire. you may want a wreath which has the two sides meeting in the center at the top, Roman-style.

If you use gilded leaves and pines, the colored bow will be a contrasting accent. However, if you work with green natural vegetation, you can use red cranberries most effectively in place of holly. Tie on a large red bow (or whatever color you want to use) made of some inexpensive ribbon, but do not stint on the bow or your wreath will look amateurish.

Idea 2: Gourds. Plant gourd seeds in your garden, if you have one. If not, buy them at a roadside market. You will be surprised at what a small, inexpensive package of seeds can do to help you earn Christmas money. Gather the gourds in the fall and bring them into your workshop. They can be dried by hanging strings around them or putting them in an old fish net. Paint the gourds in the brightest colors of lacquer you can buy. An extra coat of clear varnish, when they are dry, will enhance their beauty and make them waterproof for outside use. These gourds can be sold as "out-of-doors" decorations. They can be strung for hanging Mexican-style, in the corners of porches. Inside the house they are lovely when used in large wooden or colored bowls.

Idea 3: Sparklers. Sparklers are fun and make harmless toys for children to play with over the holidays.

To make fireworks sparklers you need:

> 10 ounces white potassium chlorate
> 2 ounces granulated aluminum
> $1/16$ ounce charcoal

Mix to a consistency of thick cream with a solution of 2 ounces of dextrin in a pint of water. Use this mixture to coat wires or wooden sticks. For red sparklers, add 1½ ounces of strontium nitrate; for green, add 2 ounces of powdered barium nitrate.

Idea 4: Paper garlands. Make paper garlands for sale.

Take a strip of crepe paper ½" wide and gather it through the center with a strong thread such as carpet thread. Push the paper along on the thread so that it is tightly gathered. Thumbtack one end of the thread securely to your table, hold the thread firmly, and start twisting the paper around and around in the same direction and you will have a beautiful garland. Cut to desired lengths, tying the string at each end. These are generally made of red or white crepe paper.

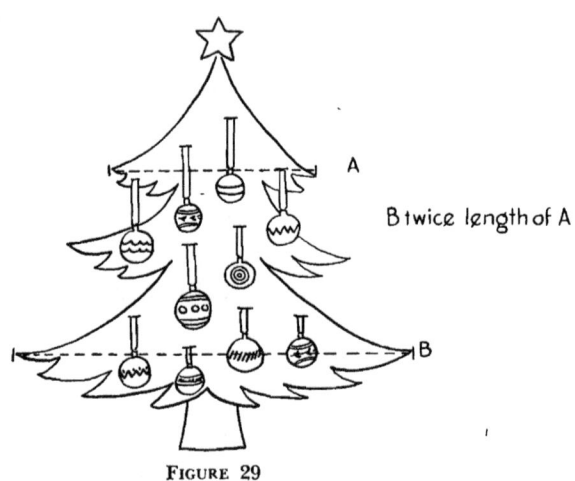

FIGURE 29

Idea 5: Miniature pipe organs. Save your father's old mailing tubes from the office; save tubes from wax paper, toilet tissue, and paper towel rolls. These can be gilded with radiator paint and allowed to dry. (Coat hangers strung on a clothesline across the room make excellent drying devices in your workshop.) The tubes can be used to make miniature pipe organs.

Other tubes can be cut into 1" lengths before painting. These you will want to paint inside as well as out. Punch a hole in the side of these "napkin-ring" sized decorations. Paint small nails and tacks with some silver and red by dipping them into the paint can. Tie them onto a thin wire and string through the punched hole.

Twenty-four Ideas for Items to Sell 109

Allow the wire ends to stick out, forming a 4" hanger. These make good Christmas tree decorations on a large tree.

Idea 6: Paper wall Christmas tree. To make cardboard cutouts of Christmas tree design (Figure 29), double a piece of newspaper as a pattern and cut out your branches—the largest one at the bottom being twice the width of the smallest at the top, which is cut to a point. Open your newspaper and lay it on a piece of green cardboard. Draw around it with a pencil. In this way, if you do not like the shape of the tree, another pattern can be cut. Make some balls out of bunched-up wet newspapers. Allow the balls to dry and then cover them with bright shades of crepe paper. You can wrap them with a string, as you do the inside of a baseball. Paste gummed gold and silver stars on these and tie them around the outside, hammock-style, leaving the ends of your string for a hanger. This string should be covered or hidden with colored satin baby ribbon. Punch small holes in your tree at various places and pull the ribbon through the hole. Scotch-tape the ribbon on the back of the tree. A paper wall tree can be used almost anywhere in the house. Be sure to put a star at the top.

Instead of balls you can make bright-colored birds. Make sausagelike bodies out of bunched-up paper and add a gumdrop for the head by sticking it on with a toothpick. Use a grain of corn for the beak and black-headed pins for the eyes. For the tail cut crepe paper 1" wide and 3" long with the grain of the paper; twist it between your fingers and glue onto the bird. Insert toothpick legs painted black. Add a ruffle around the bird's neck; make it of $1\frac{1}{2}$" wide crepe paper cut lengthwise and slit finely, like a comb. These birds can be sold separately for Christmas tree decorations.

Idea 7: Candy canes of wood. When you are collecting branches, try to find some small curved ones with a hook on the end; these make good handles for candy canes (Figure 30). Fit a branch into the end of one of your mailing tubes, and nail the two together. Paint the wood and the tube with white enamel and spiral down its length with red plastic or masking tape. Tie a red bow at the place where the two join and add some holly, evergreens, or cones.

Idea 8: Decorations of plastic foam. All kinds of decorations can be cut out of white plastic foam. This is a new material to work with, and it is lots of fun once you learn how to cut it. Make an oval-shaped piece of plastic foam 10" high for a make-believe face (Figure 31). Pin and paste on two black coat buttons for eyes, a white cotton ball for the nose, and cranberries for the mouth. For the hat cut out a piece of cardboard, like the shadow of a hat. Paint it black and add a hatband of green ribbon with a sprig of holly tacked under it. Cut another piece of cardboard in the shape of a collar. Cut a big bow tie and paint it bright red. Tack this com-

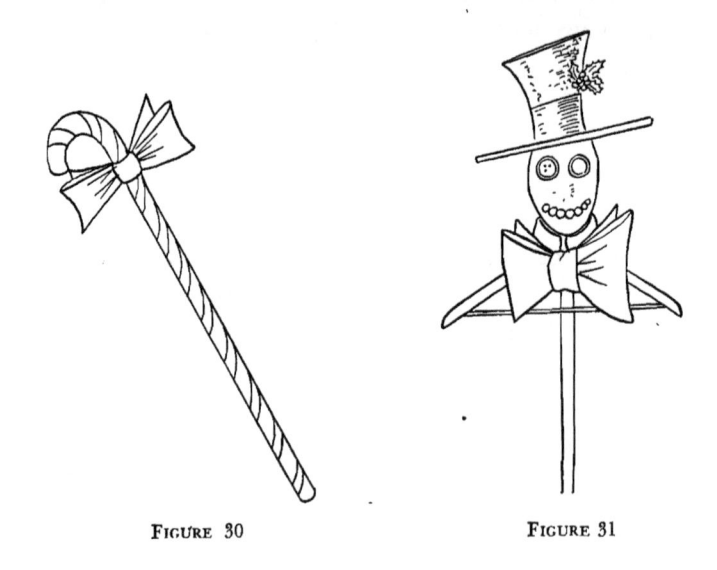

FIGURE 30   FIGURE 31

pleted head onto a stick and add a coat hanger for shoulders. You can sell this hanger to your neighbors by suggesting that they hang "one of father's coats" on it to surprise him.

Another salable idea for plastic foam is to cut star-shaped bases out of 1" thick plastic foam, making a hole in the center and using the base as a *candlestick*. Snowballs can also be cut out of plastic foam. For these you will want invisible wires. String the wire through the snowballs, using a needle. Leave enough wire to fasten onto any Christmas tree or decoration. Small stars of plastic foam make lovely tree decorations; also large ones for the top of your tree.

Twenty-four Ideas for Items to Sell 111

Silver some twopenny nails. Put one in the bottom of each V of the star. Cross a pair of nails in the center front and fasten with a string through to the back, after tying the wire over and across the nails at front center to hold them together.

Idea 9: Christmas tree decorations from old toys. Round up all the broken odds and ends of toy sets, such as checkers, one car of a toy train, a broken Ping-pong paddle, and baby blocks. Paint these in bright Christmas colors for tree decorations. They can be enhanced by the use of colored cellophane, tied with gold wrapping string or ribbon for a handle. Folks might get their old toys back and children could enjoy them all over again. This kind of work might develop into a repair shop, with business the year round.

Idea 10: Christmas tree decorations of maline. Buy some white and red maline. This is an inexpensive material that is good for making Christmas tree decorations.

Check through your magazines and find a picture of an angel; cut it out. If the angel is too small put it against a screen, and with a light behind you, cast a shadow on the wall, making the desired size, which is about 6″ in height. Have a paper handy and draw around the outline. Lay your pattern on the maline and cut around the edges. Do the same thing with pictures of birds, fish, sheep, cats, and horses; with pictures of common toys, such as rocking horses and bears; or with tree decorations, such as small Christmas trees and stars.

Use spangles (sequins) for eyes. Paint lips with nail polish and draw in the nose with a pencil. Tie a ribbon through the top center of the figure, allowing enough space for a hanger.

These maline figures make very appropriate decorations for the invalid or sickroom member of your family, as they are fresh-looking and have no odor.

Idea 11: Cardboard cutouts. Cardboard cutouts can be made in the same way as the maline figures. First paint them on both sides in bright colors. Then paste on small, irregular pieces of various colors of paper cut in geometric forms.

Idea 12: Dog's night-walk collar. Make a dog's "night walk" collar. Go to the shoe repair shop and buy a piece of leather 1" wide and as long as is needed. Buy some small glass reflectors, which shine when car lights are thrown on them at night; get small sizes of the ones used as markers on highway posts, or on signs indicating parking areas or residence drives. Brad these onto the leather strip. This is a dog's night-walk collar. It can be easily tied over his regular collar. Any dog lover who walks his dog at night on the city streets will appreciate this collar. When the country dog takes a night off, he needs it too, so that he can be easily found by the lights of a car. Sell them as a gift for Fido.

Idea 13: Glass silvered for mirrors. Silver your own glass for mirrors to be used as table decorations under flower arrangements. Use the following ingredients:

>Ammonium hydroxide, 1 part
>Silver nitrate, 2 parts
>Water, 3 parts
>Alcohol, 3 parts

Mix and dissolve these ingredients in a dim light; then filter and mix with ¼ part of corn sugar and 10 parts of alcohol (25%). Dip glass in the solution, warming it gradually to 158° F.

Idea 14: Decorations from logs or driftwood. You can make some lovely hall or mantel decorations with small logs or driftwood which were gathered out in the woods or along the seashore during the summer.

Construct a woodland scene of logs on a woven mat, which you can make from any wide, long grasses or palm fronds. Place the woven mat on a piece of flat metal or on a board so that the decoration can be removed when you sell it. Make a woods arrangement of three different-sized logs which have been prepared by dipping them in a solution of 1 part of citric acid and 3 parts of sodium bicarbonate.

Place the logs in a floral woods arrangement and add winter berries, such as sprigs of bay or holly. For a seashore arrangement, place the wood on a mirrored glass and add small shells around the

Twenty-four Ideas for Items to Sell 113

edge of the mirror, together with one large shell to hold the water for your flowers. The logs will have the foamed surface so greatly desired by garden club enthusiasts. Tell your customer that the addition of one of her porcelain figures will produce an unusual floral arrangement.

Idea 15: Shapes molded of Spanish hanging moss. If you can get Spanish hanging moss or red ground moss, treat it with soda and acid in the same manner as the logs, and mold it into unusual shapes on a large porcelain tray or mirror. Add miniature figures, such as tin soldiers and animals painted in bright colors, and you will be pleased with the results.

FIGURE 32

Idea 16: Clay figures related to hobbies. Find out your customer's favorite hobby and make miniature figures pertaining to that hobby. You can make figures of modeling clay and paint them after they have dried.

Idea 17: Rain and sunny day indicator. If you live in a rural section, a rain and sunny day indicator (Figure 32) will be useful as well as amusing. It is easy to make. All you need is a small wooden box and some kind of decorative figures, such as animals or two small dolls, 2" high, dressed in white muslin or heavy white paper. Of course, the box can be decorated in any way you wish.

Place the figures near the front of the box, or on top, just so they will be exposed to the air around them.

This is how you make the barometers. Immerse the figures of light muslin or paper in a solution of cobalt chloride, 1 part; gelatin, 10 parts; and water, 100 parts. Allow them to dry. Now the muslin or paper figures will change color as the moisture of the atmosphere changes. The normal weather color is pink, which changes into violet in medium humid weather, and into blue in very dry weather. Children love these as gifts.

Idea 18: Figurines for table and tree decorations. Make figurines of modeling clay or sculptor's putty for table or tree decorations. They are very nice for special gift packages, too.

To make modeling clay: Mix thoroughly 67 parts of clay with 33 parts of sulphur. Then mix with petrolatum in the proportion of 1 part of petrolatum to 3 parts of clay-sulphur mix.

To make sculptor's putty: Take boiled linseed oil, 15 per cent; fuller's earth, 15 per cent; and calcium carbonate, 70 per cent. Mix all these ingredients thoroughly. Mold them into the desired shapes.

Idea 19: Papier-mâché. If you need papier-mâché as a base for branches, for the floor of a crèche, or for Christmas tree balls, here is how to make it:

The materials you need are wet paper pulp (dry paper, 1 ounce; water, 3 ounces), 4 ounces; dry plaster of Paris, 8 ounces; and hot glue, ½ gill, or 4½ tablespoons. Prepare the pulp, then pour over it 3 tablespoons of hot glue and stir into a soft and very thick mass. Next add some of the plaster of Paris and mix thoroughly until the mass is so dry and thick that it can hardly be worked. Add the remainder of the glue and work up the mass again, putting in the rest of the plaster of Paris.

Idea 20: Crystallized Christmas tree. Crystallize the tree by spraying it twice with white calcium. In the second spraying add some mica flakes. Let the tree dry.

How to make mica flakes: Mix pounded fragments of mica with shellac. It forms a composition which can be molded with ease.

Twenty-four Ideas for Items to Sell 115

Idea 21: Small crocheted wreaths. Small crocheted wreaths (Figure 33) are appropriate at Christmas time for his buttonhole, her handbag or fur neckpiece, or under the bow of a gift package. These can be made in the few extra minutes you have while waiting for a phone call, waiting at the beauty parlor, or sitting in the car waiting for your best beau. You will need to buy three dozen small metal window-shade rings, one ball of green yarn, and one skein of red embroidery floss. .

To make a wreath: Thread a large-eyed, blunt needle with yarn and buttonhole-stitch around the metal ring, pushing the stitches together closely to make the ring solid. Stick your crochet needle

FIGURE 33

through the buttonhole stitch and crochet a ½" scallop chain-stitch edging, one front and one back, around the ring. Make French knots with red thread to represent holly berries. Pull red baby ribbon through the wreath at one place and tie into a small bow. Sew a little safety pin onto the back.

These crocheted wreaths are good to sell at church bazaars.

Idea 22: Rainbow-colored cones for fireplace. To make rainbow-colored cones for the fireplace, use a separate chemical for each color. Do not mix the chemicals. Apply only one color to each cone. Keep the chemicals away from children and animals, as they are poisonous! Be sure to tell your druggist you are making Christmas decorations and are using your chemicals for coloring pine cones. Use a strong solution in each case. Allow the cones to dry well before using them, or roll the cones in melted paraffin and then quickly in the dried chemicals. Be careful to dispose of your chemicals, once you have finished using them. Do not allow the solutions to stand around where they might accidentally be used for other purposes.

To make colors:

For *green* use powdered copper sulphate or barium chloride.

For *blue* use barium nitrate or copper oxide.

For *red* use strontium chloride.

FIGURE 34

For *purple* use potassium permanganate or lithium chloride (the lightest metal known).

For *violet* use magnesium chloride.

For *lavender* use potassium chloride.

For *yellow* and *orange* use soda or salt (sodium bicarbonate or sodium chloride).

Idea 23: Flower holders from stones. See if you can find some stones with deep holes worn in them. A stone 4″ or 5″ long by 2″ or 3″ wide is a good size. Be sure the hole is deep enough to

Twenty-four Ideas for Items to Sell 117

hold water for the stems of cut flowers. Now take a flower holder with metal prongs, the prongs sticking up, and cement it into the hole of the stone, using plaster of Paris on the bottom of the hole. Press the holder down with a weight until it is dry. Next take a tin pie pan and turn it upside down on a piece of glass. Cover the pie pan with moss and place the stone on the moss in a "woodsy" effect. These flower holders from stones form an effective part of many kinds of flower arrangements where an out-of-doors, woodsy scene is needed. The stones can be used throughout the year.

Idea 24: Boutonnieres. Decorated boutonnieres (Figure 34) of bright-colored flowers with green leaves can be easily made.

To make boutonnieres, use beechnut burrs which have been painted a soft green, along with pine cones painted in shades of yellow and rust.

The *rosebud boutonniere* is made of beechnuts painted in pastel shades, along with stems and leaves of corn shucks dyed a harmonizing green. Small buds made of corn shucks can be dyed yellow. Buds made of organdy in various pastel shades can be substituted.

The *acorn boutonniere* can be made of acorns painted in any bright fall color, along with leaves and stems of corn shucks dyed brown.

The *spruce cone boutonniere* is made with small cones painted in winter shades, with brown corn shucks for leaves and stems.

Any of these boutonnieres make lovely decorations for place cards at the luncheon or dinner table.

INDEX

Anniversaries, wedding, 84-85

Baby showers, 86
Ballroom, decorating, 86-87
Basket for Christmas greens, 72
Bedroom, 74-76
Bedroom door, 74-75
Bird cage for Christmas greens, 72
Birthday, November, 82
Bookcase, 72
Book markers, 71-72
Boutonnieres, 117
Boys' party, Christmas table for, 61-62
Bridal showers, 83
Buffet supper, 85

Calendar, flower, 91-92
Candleholders, 67-68
Candy canes
  stovepipe, 68-69
  of wood, 109
Cardboard cutouts, 111
Children's parties, 81-83
Christmas, 25-77
Christmas cards, 46-47
Christmas table
  for boys' party, 61-62
  for girls' party, 62-66
Christmas tree
  crystallized, 114
  for living room, 45-46
  out-of-doors, 77
  wall, 57-61
Christmas tree decorations, 111
Church, 91-92
Circus party, 82-83
Clay figures, 113
Club, 93-94
Collar, dog's, 112
Color in flowers, 98
Cones for fireplace, 115
Crèche, 48
Crocheted wreaths, 115
Crystallized Christmas tree, 114
Cutouts, 111

Decorating for money, 103-17
Della Robbia wreaths, 66-68
Desk, 51
Dining room, 57-69
  during club meeting, 93-94
  planning decorations for, 57
  living room and, decorations between, 48-49
  table and chairs in, 59-61
  wall Christmas trees for, 57-61
Dog's collar, 112
Door
  of bedroom, 74-75
  front, 26-36

Door (continued)
  to kitchen, 68-69
  trees for, 36
Door sprays, 31-32
Doorway, garland over, 48-49
Doorway decorations for living room, 46-47
Driftwood, 112-13

Easter, 10-12
Easter tree, 10-12
Egg, tree, 11-12
Entrance hall, 40-45
  during club meeting, 93
Evergreens, 43-45
  homemade, 49

Fan, gold, 42-43
  on mantel, 52-53
Father's Day, 14
Favors, lollipop, 64-66
Figurines, 114
Fireplace
  cones for, 115
  crèche in, 48
Fisherman's mantel, 53-54
Floor lamp, 50
Flower calendar, 91-92
Flower arrangements, 97-99; see also text discussion under individual occasions
  fragrances and colors in, 98
  kinds of, 97-98
  for outdoor table, 100
  precautions in, 98-99
Flower holders, 116-17
Flowers, lengthening life of, 99
Foam, plastic, 110-11
Fourth of July, 14-15
Fragrances, 98
Front door, 26-36

Garland
  over doorway, 48-49
  paper, 108
Getting started, 105
Gift table, 50
Girls' party, Christmas table for, 62-66
Glass, silvering, 112
Glorified Della Robbia wreath, 68
Gold fan, 42-43
  on mantel, 52-53
Golden wedding anniversary, 85
Good luck piece, 41-42
Gourds, 107
Greens, basket or bird cage for, 72
Gymnasium, decorating, 86-87

Hall
  to dining room during club meeting, 94
  entrance, 40-45, 93
Hall stairway, 37-40
Halloween, 15-18

119

Hat, stovepipe, 9-10
Hobbies, clay figures related to, 113
Holly, homemade, 49
Holly wreaths, 49
House plants, 49

Ideas for items to sell, 105-17
Independence Day, 14-15

Jolly front door decoration, 35-36

Kitchen, 69-71

Lamp, floor, 50
Library, 71-73
Living room, 45-55
  Christmas tree for, 45-46
  and dining room, decorations between, 48-49
  desk in, 51
  doorway decorations for, 46-47
  walls of, 51
  window of, 47-48
Logs, decorations from, 112-13
Lollipop favors, 64-66

Maline, 111
Mantel, 51-53
  fisherman's, 53-54
  gold fan on, 52-53
Mantel trees, 51-52
Mirrors, silvering, 112
Mistletoe, 44-45
Money, earning, 103-17
Mother's Day, 12-14
Music box, 73-74
Music room, 73-74
Musical stairway, 38-40

New Year's Day, 3-5
Night-walk collar, 112
November birthday, 82

Organs, 40-41, 108-9

Package, 104
Paper garlands, 108
Papier-mâché, 114
Perseverance, 105
Personal qualifications, 104
Pillows, sofa, 49
Pineapple candleholders, 67-68
Pipe organs, 40-41, 108-9
Plants, 49
Plastic foam, 110-11
Popcorn balls, 70-71
Powder room, tree for, 55-57
President's table, 93
Product, 104
Production, 104
Profit, 104-5
Proms, 86-87

Qualifications, 104

Reception, wedding, 84

Safety, 77
St. Patrick's Day, 8-10
St. Valentine's Day, 5-8
Shadow box, 6
Showers
  baby, 86
  bridal, 83
Silver wedding anniversary, 84-85
Sofa pillows, 49
Spanish moss, 113
Sparklers, 107-8
Speakers' room, 93
Speakers' table, 94
Special occasions, 81-87
Sprays, door, 31-32
Stairway, hall, 37-40
  musical, 38-40
Stars, 32-34
  across window, 47-48
Starting, 105
Stone flower holders, 116
Stovepipe candy canes, 68-69
Stovepipe hat, 9-10
Success, 104
Supper, buffet, 85

Tables
  Christmas, 59-60, 61-66
  for club meeting, 94
  gift, 50
  outside, 100
Television party, 15
Thanksgiving Day, 18-21
Toys, old, 111
Tree egg, 11-12
Trees
  for door, 36
  Easter, 10-12
  mantel, 51-52
  powder room, 55-57

Valentine's Day, 5-8
Vegetable garden, 100

Walls of living room, 51
Wastebaskets, 49
Weather indicator, 113-14
Wedding, 83-84
Wedding anniversaries, 84-85
Wedding reception, 84
Windows
  living-room, 47-48
  kitchen, 70
Wreaths
  crocheted, 115
  Della Robbia, 66-68
  holly, 49
  large, 26-29
  to sell, 105-7
  small, 29-30

Yard, 76-77